KITCHEN & BATH
DESIGN PRINCIPLES

KITCHEN & BATH
DESIGN PRINCIPLES
Elements, Form, Styles

Second Edition

NANCY L. WOLFORD, PhD

ELLEN CHEEVER, CMKBD, ASID, CAPS

National Kitchen & Bath Association

Cover image: Kitchen design by Brigitte C. Fabi, CMKBD. Photo by Eric Hausman
Bathroom design by Lilley E. Yee, CMKBD, CID, ASID. Photo Copyright Dean J. Birinyi, ASMP

Cover design: Wiley

This book is printed on acid-free paper. ∞

Copyright © 2015 by John Wiley & Sons, Inc. All rights reserved.

Published by John Wiley & Sons, Inc., Hoboken, New Jersey.

Published simultaneously in Canada.

No part of this publication may be reproduced, stored in a retrieval system, or transmitted in any form or by any means, electronic, mechanical, photocopying, recording, scanning, or otherwise, except as permitted under Section 107 or 108 of the 1976 United States Copyright Act, without either the prior written permission of the Publisher, or authorization through payment of the appropriate per-copy fee to the Copyright Clearance Center, 222 Rosewood Drive, Danvers, MA 01923, (978) 750-8400, fax (978) 646-8600, or on the web at www.copyright.com. Requests to the Publisher for permission should be addressed to the Permissions Department, John Wiley & Sons, Inc., 111 River Street, Hoboken, NJ 07030, (201) 748-6011, fax (201) 748-6008, or online at www.wiley.com/go/permissions.

Limit of Liability/Disclaimer of Warranty: While the publisher and author have used their best efforts in preparing this book, they make no representations or warranties with the respect to the accuracy or completeness of the contents of this book and specifically disclaim any implied warranties of merchantability or fitness for a particular purpose. No warranty may be created or extended by sales representatives or written sales materials. The advice and strategies contained herein may not be suitable for your situation. You should consult with a professional where appropriate. Neither the publisher nor the author shall be liable for damages arising herefrom.

For general information about our other products and services, please contact our Customer Care Department within the United States at (800) 762-2974, outside the United States at (317) 572-3993 or fax (317) 572-4002.

Wiley publishes in a variety of print and electronic formats and by print-on-demand. Some material included with standard print versions of this book may not be included in e-books or in print-on-demand. If this book refers to media such as a CD or DVD that is not included in the version you purchased, you may download this material at http://booksupport.wiley.com. For more information about Wiley products, visit www.wiley.com.

Library of Congress Cataloging-in-Publication Data:

Wolford, Nancy L.
  Kitchen & bath design principles : elements, form, styles / Nancy L. Wolford, Ellen Cheever. — Second Edition.
      pages cm
    Includes index.
    ISBN 978-1-118-71568-0 (cloth); 978-1-118-71564-2 (ebk.); 978-1-118-71565-9 (ebk.)
    1. Kitchens. 2. Bathrooms. I. Cheever, Ellen. II. Title. III. Title: Kitchen and bath design principles.
    NK2117.K5W65 2014
    747.7'8—dc23
                                                            2014034571
Printed in the United States of America

V10019390_062420

Sponsors

The National Kitchen & Bath Association recognizes with gratitude Delta Faucet Company, whose generous contribution supported the development of this second edition of *Design Principles*.

GOLD SPONSOR

DELTA FAUCET COMPANY

About the National Kitchen & Bath Association

The National Kitchen & Bath Association (NKBA) is the only nonprofit trade association dedicated exclusively to the kitchen and bath industry and is the leading source of information and education for professionals in the field. Fifty years after its inception, the NKBA has a membership of more than 55,000 and is the proud owner of the Kitchen & Bath Industry Show (KBIS).

The NKBA's mission is to enhance member success and excellence, promote professionalism and ethical business practices, and provide leadership and direction for the kitchen and bath industry worldwide.

The NKBA has pioneered innovative industry research, developed effective business management tools, and set groundbreaking design standards for safe, functional, and comfortable kitchens and baths.

Recognized as the kitchen and bath industry's leader in learning and professional development, the NKBA offers professionals of all levels of experience essential reference materials, conferences, virtual learning opportunities, marketing assistance, design competitions, consumer referrals, internships, and opportunities to serve in leadership positions.

The NKBA's internationally recognized certification program provides professionals the opportunity to demonstrate knowledge and excellence as Associate Kitchen & Bath Designer (AKBD), Certified Kitchen Designer (CKD), Certified Bath Designer (CBD), and Certified Master Kitchen & Bath Designer (CMKBD).

For students entering the industry, the NKBA offers Accredited and Supported Programs, which provide NKBA-approved curriculum at more than 60 learning institutions throughout the United States and Canada.

For consumers, the NKBA showcases award-winning designs and provides information on remodeling, green design, safety, and more at NKBA.org. The NKBA Pro Search tool helps consumers locate kitchen and bath professionals in their area.

The NKBA offers membership in 11 different industry segments: dealers, designers, manufacturers and suppliers, multi-branch retailers and home centers, decorative plumbing and hardware, manufacturer's representatives, builders and remodelers, installers, fabricators, cabinet shops, and distributors. For more information, visit NKBA.org.

Contents

Preface

*Aesthetics and style in design are as important
as functional space planning in kitchens and bathrooms.*

Today, the consumer's definition of good design in residential kitchen and bathroom planning places equal importance on function, style, and beauty.

- Consumers expect the kitchen and bathroom to look good as well as be functional. One aspect of the plan is not given up for the other.
- Consumers pride themselves in planning their own kitchen or bathroom; however, they expect the kitchen/bath specialist to help them create a personalized, one-of-a-kind space.
- Consumers who desire luxury products as well as those on a more modest budget are interested in good style and design. Their appreciation of style and design has grown from exposure to well-designed home products, including those created by recognized designers, artists, or home fashion experts in retail stores, on television decorating shows, and on the Internet.

To meet this professional challenge and provide design excellence, both experienced and novice designers need to expand their planning expertise to encompass the elements and principles of design as well as a variety of historical or specific cultural design trends and themes, often requested by today's clients. Doing this requires both academic study and the ability to think beyond the industry standard of covering the walls with well-engineered cabinets and specifying highly functional, well-made manufactured materials, fixtures, and appliances to create an aesthetically pleasing, creative, and personalized kitchen and/or bathroom.

The primary focus of this volume of the NKBA Professional Resource Library is on the planning of the physical appearance of the kitchen and bathroom. Included is a brief history of the design of kitchens and bathrooms (chapter 1) as well as some basics of creating a design, using skill and creativity to personalize designs for clients (chapter 2). It explains and details how to apply the academic elements (chapter 3) and principles (chapter 4) of design and selected historic and cultural style themes to specific kitchen and bathroom situations, enabling the designer to more clearly understand how to apply these tools of design to daily business practice. The historic and cultural style themes are presented as chronologically as possible. Those through and up to the end of the nineteenth century are discussed in chapter 5; those through the late nineteenth, through the twentieth and into the beginning of the twenty-first century in chapter 6, with selected cultural style themes presented in chapter 7. Although references to the design planning process, kitchen and bathroom layouts, types of equipment, and various materials are made, the major thrust of this volume is how the kitchen or bathroom visually presents itself to the customer using and enjoying the space. New and expanded illustrations of the application of each of these concepts to kitchens and bathrooms are included to enhance your knowledge and skill as a designer and serve as reference points and real-life examples to use when creating designs and working with clients.

For the design student and designers preparing for the AKBD Exam, this volume addresses the following selected competencies in the NKBA Body of Knowledge:

Body of Knowledge Competency: Design
5. Design Principles: Demonstrates knowledge of color theories and how color relates to space (chapter 3).
6. Design Principles: Demonstrates design solutions using the elements and principles of design to satisfy aesthetic criteria (chapters 3 and 4).
7. Kitchen Planning & Bath Planning: Demonstrates knowledge of kitchen and bath historical styles and shows awareness of current design trends (chapters 1, 5, 6, and 7).
8. Kitchen Planning & Bath Planning: Evaluates client needs and incorporates them in the design solution (chapters 2, 5, 6, and 7).

This volume also addresses the following selected CIDA Professional Standards 2014:

II. Interior Design: Critical Thinking, Professional Values, and Processes

Standard 2: Global Perspective for Design—Have a global view and weigh design decisions within the parameters of . . . cultural context) (chapter 7).

Standard 4: Design Process—Apply all aspects of the design process to creative problem solving . . . and generate creative solutions that optimize the human experience within the interior environment) (chapter 2).

III. Interior Design: Core Design and Technical Knowledge

Standard 8: History—Apply knowledge of interiors, architecture, decorative arts, and art within a historical and cultural context) (chapters 1, 5, and 6).

Standard 9: Space and Form—Apply elements and principles of two- and three-dimensional design (chapters 3 and 4).

Standard 10: Color—Apply color principles and theories (chapters 3 and 4).

There is an abundance of information included in this volume, meant to serve as a reference when working with clients. My hope is that it will increase and enhance your knowledge and skill as a designer. Enjoy design and creating those perfect kitchen and bathroom spaces for your clients, whatever the style or theme.

It was an honor to be asked to revise this volume, a culmination of more than 40 years of college teaching: interior design theory and history along with space planning and other interior design courses. These basic design concepts (elements and principles of design) are the backbone and building blocks of any designed space, including kitchens and bathrooms. The trend to restore, re-create, or create the feeling of a historical space to complement exterior architectural and interior style has increased in recent years, so much so that it became an integral part of my teaching in the history of interiors and space planning classes. Students have enjoyed the challenge of applying this historical and theme aspect to their design projects and have been inspirations. My thanks to them.

Many contributors made this book possible. Special thanks go to Johanna Baars, Publications Specialist at NKBA; Paul Drougas, Editor, and Michael New, Editorial Assistant at John Wiley & Sons; Ellen Cheever, CMKBD, ASID, author of the first edition; the designers whose projects illustrate the design elements, principles, themes, and styles; and the peer reviewers who provided useful comments and suggestions. Finally, special thanks to my husband and family for their encouragement, support, and patience throughout this process.

Acknowledgments

The NKBA gratefully acknowledges the following peer reviewers of this book:

Sharon L. Flatley, CMKBD, ASID

Geeta Kewalramani, CMKBD

Julie Myers, AKBD, ASID, NCIDQ

Arlynne Wolf, CKD (deceased)

A Brief History of Kitchen and Bathroom Design

It is important for the kitchen and bath designer to understand the historical background of the design of the residential kitchen and bathroom in the United States and how it evolved. These spaces are often taken for granted as being primarily functional, necessary, and convenient rooms that have always been indoors, as they have been in most Western homes for a century or more. Fewer and fewer customers or designers can remember having or using primitive outdoor spaces for these functions, except when hiking or camping or in extremely remote areas. Therefore, giving thought to the actual design of these spaces is a relatively new concept, yet it is an opportunity for the expertise of the kitchen and bath designer.

Learning Objective 1: Describe the development and evolution of the design of the residential kitchen.

Learning Objective 2: Describe the development and evolution of the design of the residential bathroom.

A BRIEF HISTORY OF THE KITCHEN

For many centuries of recorded history, the kitchen was outside or in a separate building apart from the primary home to protect the family's dwelling from fires. The kitchen eventually became attached to the dwelling but was considered by most to be strictly a separate functional work space rather than one that required designing, aesthetic considerations, or integration into the rest of the house. This was especially true for the wealthy, who often had staff handling the meal preparation and cleanup. Aesthetics, close or convenient location to eating/dining space, or ease of function were not considered, nor were they thought to be important. In Colonial America in the seventeenth and eighteenth centuries and into the nineteenth century, the kitchen became more integrated into the home, more a center of family life with the open flame from the fireplace used to warm the home and family as well as prepare the food. The kitchen of the Rundlet-May House (1807) in Portsmouth, New Hampshire, features an enclosed fireplace—an early forerunner of the modern kitchen stove (see Figure 1.1.)

The idea of a well-planned, well-designed kitchen was first talked about in the 1920s when Hoosier cabinets were introduced by the Hoosier Company. Later, Cornell University and the US Department of Agriculture Research Station in Beltsville, Maryland, began research on

FIGURE 1.1 Historical kitchen
Courtesy of the Society of Preservation of New England Antiquities
Photo by David Bohl

functional kitchen planning. This research continued after World War II by the Small Homes Council of the University of Illinois at Urbana-Champaign. However, the room still remained primarily a workroom, where function (food preparation, storage, and cleanup), mass production of cabinetry, and ease of cleaning, rather than aesthetics or other uses, were the primary considerations (see Figure 1.2).

Immediately following World War II, several leading midwestern and eastern US cabinet companies introduced color and more wood for cabinetry, which gradually was becoming built in, as well as decorative hardware and a variety of accent cabinet pieces. Built-in appliances and fixtures were introduced in the late 1950s and 1960s, in a myriad of styles and colors. These avant-garde kitchens were widely shown in high-fashion magazines, such as *Town & Country* and *Vogue*, as well as the many home design shelter publications that were popular and widely read by consumers (see Figure 1.3).

In the 1970s, a new design concept was introduced in several well-respected shelter magazines—the great room. Walls were removed between the kitchen and adjacent living spaces, bringing the kitchen out of the strictly separate functional/work-oriented category, to become an integral part of the family public/social space. It also helped to make homes appear to be larger as some walls were removed. The concept of the great room brought mass appeal to the idea of a decorated kitchen—one that was attractive to look at as well as functional to work and entertain in and continues to be popular (see Figure 1.4).

"WHERE OUR WORK IS, THERE LET OUR JOY BE"

A KITCHEN that is pleasant and easy to work in spreads harmony throughout the home. There, where so many important household tasks are performed, first rate plumbing is an essential key to cleanliness, health and convenience. *Kohler quality* costs no more and gives the protection of excellence in every detail.

The Wilshire sink, illustrated above, with its two compartments, double drainboard and handy ledge, typifies the practical design and distinguished appearance of all Kohler fixtures and fittings. The rigid, durable cast iron construction is overlaid with a pure white, lustrous surface, easy to clean, and

acid resisting clear through the enamel. The working parts are designed, constructed and tested with utmost care to assure ease, precision and reliability in performance. Kohler quality is safeguarded by the fact that Kohler products are made in one plant, under one supervision.

Your Master Plumber will gladly explain the enduring benefits and built-in values of Kohler plumbing. Consult him for valuable help in selecting fixtures and fittings for a new or remodeled kitchen, bathroom, washroom or laundry. Send for booklet HB-9, "Planned Bathrooms and Kitchens." Kohler Co., Kohler, Wisconsin. Established 1873.

Buy and Keep
U. S. War Bonds

KOHLER of KOHLER

MBING FIXTURES AND FITTINGS • HEATING EQUIPMENT • ELECTRIC PLANTS

FIGURE 1.2 1940s kitchen

Courtesy of Kohler Company

FIGURE 1.3 1960s kitchen
Courtesy of Sub Zero

The concept of an aesthetically pleasing kitchen (whether a separate space or part of the great room concept) grew in importance throughout the 1970s, 1980s, and into the 1990s as the English bespoke idea of an unfitted kitchen was coupled with consumer interest in highly stylized, traditionally influenced environments attempting to re-create the warmth of a sundrenched villa in Tuscany, a colonial cottage in New England, or the midcentury modern look. Architectural details from these historic or period settings became more and more popular for consumers planning kitchens that were becoming the center of activity in their homes. A traditional kitchen with Old World design details is still popular today (see Figure 1.5).

The concept of a kitchen outdoors returned in the early 2000s, although it is quite different from the simple fire pits or crude adobe ovens of earlier times. This concept created a new wealth of design opportunities for the kitchen designer. The outdoor kitchens range from simple built-in barbecues to elaborate structures that are as extensive, complete, and well thought-out and designed as typical indoor kitchens (see Figure 1.6).

The interest in such aesthetically pleasing spaces continues today. As a kitchen specialist, one may be asked to plan a room that has a European-influenced sleek, uncluttered, and sophisticated style; a mid-twentieth-century modern renovation, or one that is harmonious and calming, inspired by a Far Eastern interior. The designer's ability to appropriately use the elements and principles of good design as well as understand historic and cultural themes will add great value to functional space planning solutions. Contemporary kitchens today combine convenience, function, and beauty. In the example shown in Figure 1.7, plain, simple

FIGURE 1.4 Great room/kitchen design concept introduced in the 1970s
Design by Carol Swanson-Petterson, CKD; KB Cabinets, Millbrae, CA

cabinets are highlighted with sleek cabinet pulls. Relatively smooth and varied wood-grained countertops and stainless-steel appliances are contrasted with the rough-textured wall treatment.

A BRIEF HISTORY OF THE BATHROOM

For most of recorded history, the bathroom, as it is known today, did not exist. The outhouse or any convenient outdoor space was the toilet norm, as were outdoor washing facilities, often a stream or other body of water. However, indoor bath spaces strictly for bathing in some sort of tub or with a pitcher and bowl for washing have been around since ancient Greek and Roman times. It took centuries for these activities to come together in a single space. Although luxury homes featured indoor bathrooms with plumbed fixtures in the late 1800s, it was not until the 1920s that most building codes began mandating indoor plumbing for all new residential construction. These new codes paid little attention to the way the bathroom looked or how much space was required, because the space was perceived primarily as utilitarian. At first for typical bathrooms, few choices existed for fixture styles, colors, or fitting finishes. The primary concerns of

FIGURE 1.5 Traditional 1990s kitchen

Design by Bryan Reiss, CMKBD and Scott Stultz, codesigners Peter Deane and Kelly Stewart, CMKBD

early bathroom planners were providing safe indoor water supply intake and removal and accommodating three basic, usually white, fixtures in the smallest space possible. They also converted a dressing room, nursery, or other small room that had sufficient space for fixtures (see Figure 1.8).

Although many builders, designers, and architects overlooked the potential beauty of the bathroom, American filmmakers and emerging design trendsetters realized how attractive a bathroom could be. Sets in the emerging Hollywood film industry during the 1920s and 1930s suggested the potential beauty and luxury of the bathroom. Major manufacturers expanded their product lines and introduced color in their fixtures. An early Kohler advertisement celebrates this use of color in the bathroom (see Figure 1.9).

In 1929, the New York Metropolitan Museum of Art featured an exhibit devoted to the artistic and aesthetic qualities of a residential household, including the bathroom, using black fixtures to contrast with the light tile (see Figure 1.10).

During and immediately after World War II, the use of American-made fixtures was emphasized, and pastel colors were introduced. The advertisement in Figure 1.11 from the *Saturday Evening Post* in 1948 illustrates this use of color.

In the 1950s, 1960s, and 1970s, along with an explosion of the use of color for bathroom fixtures, greater use of color for floor and surrounding wall materials also occurred. The

FIGURE 1.6 Outdoor kitchen
Courtesy of Lynx Grills, Inc.

customer (and designer) had many choices, beyond white or the pastels of the era through the 1940s. These colors changed from decade to decade, as the three advertisements in Figures 1.12, 1.13, and 1.14 illustrate with different versions of green.

The fantasies of trendsetters and the explosion in the use of color all those years ago are the reality for well-planned bathrooms today. No longer is the bathroom a room reserved for simple personal hygiene. Today, people spend more time in the space. Some gather in a family group to enjoy the therapeutic pleasure of a hydromassage bath sauna, soaking tub, or steam shower; others use the bathroom as a secluded spot, a place to relax and unwind, away from hectic family and job responsibilities.

As a bathroom specialist, you may be asked to plan a room that is part of a major luxury master bedroom suite or one that is a separate, compartmentalized, multifunctional room. Your client may request a dramatic powder room reserved primarily for guests, a shower space squeezed off the utility room, or an outdoor cabana by the swimming pool.

In all of these situations, the ability to use the elements and principles of good design adds great aesthetic value to the functional space planning solution for today's client (see Figure 1.15).

FIGURE 1.7 Contemporary European-influenced kitchen
Design by German Brun, LEED, AP, codesigner Lizmarie Esparza; Den Architecture, Miami, FL
Photo by Greg Clark

FIGURE 1.8 Historical bathroom, early twentieth century
Courtesy of Kohler Company

For bathrooms *glorious* in color

America discovered the bathroom—and glorified it! And now comes Kohler Colorware, bestowing upon this room an added charm and dignity. Now bathrooms may be glorious in color. With fixtures in beautiful shades of lavender, blue, ivory, brown, green, gray—delicate yet everlastingly permanent . . .

Different bathrooms, you will perceive, may be done in different color schemes, each with its individual charm and character. Tub,

lavatory, toilet—all contribute to the harmonious ensemble, for Kohler fixtures in both enamel and vitreous ware are now made in color. Kohler fittings in softly lustrous chromium plate add the final touch of perfection.

Color means Kohler. To appreciate this new beauty you must see Kohler fixtures. Visit a Kohler showroom if you can—for a true aesthetic thrill. And consult your plumber. He will tell you that a bathroom

in Kohler Colorware costs little more than one in white...Mail the coupon for glimpses of bathrooms in *all* the Kohler Colors.

KOHLER CO., Kohler, Wis.
Gentlemen: Please send me your booklet of plumbing fixtures in color—"Color Charm Enters the Bathroom."

Name
Street Address
City   State

KOHLER CO., Founded 1873, KOHLER, WIS.   Shipping Point, Sheboygan, Wis.   Branches in Principal Cities

KOHLER OF KOHLER
Plumbing Fixtures
LOOK FOR THE KOHLER TRADE MARK ON EACH FIXTURE

FIGURE 1.9 Historical bathroom, 1920s, introducing color
Courtesy of Kohler Company

In the Metropolitan Museum of Art
—Exhibition of a modern bath and dressing room

THE new importance of the bathroom as a place of beauty in the modern home could hardly be more strikingly emphasized than it is by this room by Mr. Ely Jacques Kahn in the current Exhibition of American Industrial Art at the Metropolitan Museum, New York.

That the bathroom was chosen as one of the typical rooms to be shown in this internationally important exhibition is in itself an eloquent fact. The manner in which this room unites artistry with logical simplicity demonstrates the wisdom of the choice.

The walls are of glass. The floors are of special yielding rubber. Radiators are recessed behind tiled grilles, and over their warmth

hang the towels. Such thoughtful details throughout illustrate how comfort parallels beauty.

Into this setting are introduced a Kohler bath and lavatory of gleaming black, with chromium-plated fittings—faucets, handles, and escutcheons—also of Kohler make, in the graceful *Cellini* design. These Kohler contributions are in patterns available to all.

Kohler fixtures of modern style and beauty—in lovely color or lustrous white—are made for simplest bathrooms as well as costly ones. Write to Kohler Co., Kohler, Wis., for a free 72-page book, in color, showing fixtures for bathrooms, kitchens, and laundries, with color schemes, floor plans, and prices.

KOHLER CO. Founded 1873 · Branches in Principal Cities · Shipping Point, Sheboygan, Wis.

KOHLER OF KOHLER
Plumbing Fixtures

FIGURE 1.10 1929 MMA bathroom exhibit by Kohler
Courtesy of Kohler Company

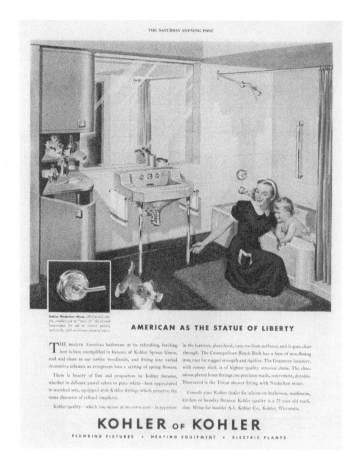

FIGURE 1.11 1940s historical bathroom ad
Courtesy of Kohler Company

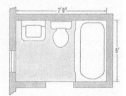

FIGURE 1.12 1950s spruce green
bathroom ad
Courtesy of Kohler Company

FIGURE 1.13 1960s bathroom ad
Courtesy of Kohler Company

FIGURE 1.14 1970s avocado bathroom fixtures ad
Courtesy of Kohler Company

FIGURE 1.15 Bathroom from today
Design by Elizabeth A. Rosensteel; Elizabeth A. Rosensteel Design/Studio, Phoenix, AZ.
Photo by Robert Reck

SUMMARY

This chapter presents a brief history of the design of kitchens and bathrooms in the United States and how they changed, providing the background to assist the designer when working with these spaces with clients.

REVIEW QUESTIONS

1. Describe the development of design in the kitchen over the last 50 years. (See "Brief History of the Kitchen" pages 1–5)
2. What are some of the important milestones in the evolution of bathroom design? (See "Brief History of the Bathroom" pages 5–7)

Basics of Design: Creating Customized Design

People often mistakenly believe that designers automatically have a knack—a natural talent—for design. Although a natural affinity—a discerning eye—is definitely an asset and part of a good designer's ability, leaders in this industry, as well as educators in the field of interior design or space planning, agree that understanding and applying accepted guidelines is the foundation of an individual's basic skill set. These guidelines are known as the elements and principles of design.

Experience within the design field leads to the development of a sense of style, and that sense of style is much more difficult to categorize than a rule-based formula, often referred to as skill. An individual's ability to think creatively beyond the boundaries of accepted ideas leads to personalized, unique solutions appropriate for each client's home. Therefore, first designers must learn the rules—the elements and principles of design—that serve as a foundation for their skill as designers. Mastering these guidelines, combined with keen observation and experience, increases designers' ability to think beyond the ordinary and to develop creativity and the ability to personalize designs for clients.

> *Learning Objective 1: Describe the specific information that needs to be gathered from the client to begin a design project.*
>
> *Learning Objective 2: Explain how a designer can create a personalized and unique space for the client.*
>
> *Learning Objective 3: Describe what design skills are, and explain how to assist clients in developing their own design style.*
>
> *Learning Objective 4: Describe how one develops creativity and applies it to design solutions.*

SKILL IS THE EXECUTOR OF A DESIGN PROGRAM

The designer's skill and style direct the design effort. Skill is the designer's ability to select the best choice from several acceptable alternatives that work for the client and the specific situation. This skill is usually acquired in several different ways, including academic knowledge, observation, and practical experience, often trial and error at first. Figure 2.1 shows an example of a bathroom, skillfully created and with a sense of style. The contrast of the black-and-white marble floor tiles combined with a symmetrically balanced vanity wall of wood paneling makes this personal space feel like a library.

FIGURE 2.1 The basics of beauty: A setting created by designer Oscar Shamaniam, titled *Le Bain Parc Monseau*, at the Kohler Design Center
Courtesy of Kohler Company

Developing Design Style

Developing a design style takes experience based extensively on observation. The best way to begin is to become more visually aware of good design, which is around one all the time and derive inspiration from it. To do so:

- **Look at a garden as a whole composition.** For example—colors, line, balance, and emphasis.
- **When watching television, study the commercials and show sets.** The clothes probably are coordinated with the background set. Lighting and color may play a key part in establishing a focal point.
- **Stop and admire window displays in storefronts.** The balance, rhythm, and color combinations are often just the beginning of these highly styled vignettes and can serve as design inspiration; take photographs to serve as inspiration.
- **Gather examples of good design and trends in the industry.** Study kitchen and bathroom designs in consumer and trade magazines. Check both print and the numerous Internet sites and blogs devoted to home design as well as those of respected manufacturers and shelter magazines. Note how the details of the spaces are woven together. Some designers still tear out magazine pages that feature great examples but today, more and more, designers are saving these images digitally and categorizing them electronically in a variety of ways, including organizing them in an digital folder for a specific client or on one of the many design idea websites.

- **Visit showrooms, designer home tours, and showcase houses.** Evaluate how the spaces are laid out and the products are combined. Look closely for small design details. With permission, take photographs of spaces you like. Also invest in your own education by purchasing good books (either print or digital) featuring kitchen and bath designs and attending trade shows where products are displayed and new products are introduced—it is important to see the actual item. You can learn about design, from a skill and a style standpoint—as well as product features and benefits in these settings created by masterful merchandisers.

Creativity: Is It a Natural Gift, or Can It Be Learned?

As Kathleen Donohue, CMKBD, a noted northwestern designer, once said, "The prevailing opinion in our society is that creativity and a flair for design are inherent abilities that either one has or does not have. Because creativity is so often (and I firmly believe incorrectly) regarded as a subjective ability that cannot be measured quantitatively, kitchen and bath specialists tend to be at their least confident when a client asks about color, fabric, or specific styles appropriate to the kitchen, which has been carefully created from a functional standpoint by the designer." Some designers may worry because they are not sure if they are creative. Will their recommendations be based simply on their own personal taste?

For the kitchen and bathroom designer, creativity can probably best be defined as presenting a workable solution in an unusual yet practical and functional way. Winners in the industry understand the true definition of creativity: "Creativity is the emergence of something new which is relative, useful, or important."

The word "new" is not to be construed as something never in existence before; rather, "new" generally means an accumulation of knowledge coming together in a unique manner to supply an answer not thought of or reached before or a solution not tried in the past. Therefore, the ability to be creative is not limited to a natural talent that allows one to do something never conceived before; rather, it is the dedication to continually search for variations in the way space is treated.

The foundation of creativity is critical thinking, diligence, perseverance, and dedication; thinking of all the possible solutions for a given situation. All individuals have the potential to be creative. As one steps beyond the basics of kitchen and bath functional planning, learning the elements and principles of design and the basic historic and cultural design themes appropriate for creating stylized rooms, one is developing a skill level that will lead to increasing creative thinking abilities—and confidence in design as well.

Definition of Good Design

After establishing the differences among learned skill, acquired style, and creativity, it is still worthwhile pondering the question: What is a simple definition of good design?

A Unified Look

Masters in the design field agree that the most important part of any room is that it has a unified look. The key to a unified look is how each individual part of the room relates to the others and to the whole room. Unity of design does not mean the entire room must be the same—the same color, the same style, the same material. Far from it. Indeed, eclectic combinations of unusual and dissimilar items are very popular today.

Rather, unity of design means that all dissimilar items or elements of the space are visually tied together in an organized, logical, balanced yet interesting way. Here, again, is where knowing the rules—the elements and principles of design—assists newcomers down the path toward success and reinvigorates veterans in the industry who are looking for ways to refresh their approach to kitchen and/or bath planning. (See Figures 2.2 and 2.3 as examples.)

TABLE 2.1 Client Profile Survey Form

Design Aesthetics and Theme Criteria—Kitchen and Bathroom

1. HOUSE STYLE

EXTERIOR ARCHITECTURAL STYLE

    Is the home historic?

    What time period?

    Any historic, covenants, or deed restrictions?

NATURE OF PROJECT:

    Renovation?

    Return to original?

    New construction?

DEGREE OF ACCURACY/AUTHENTICITY DESIRED:

2. INTERIOR ARCHITECTURE AND FURNITURE STYLE:

INTERIOR AND FURNITURE STYLE PREFERENCES:

COLLECTIONS/ACCESSORIES FOR USE IN SPACE:

INSPIRATION PIECES OR PHOTOS?

COLOR PREFERENCES:

    Existing colors that can't be changed:

    Favorites:

    Color(s) to avoid:

PATTERN /MOTIF PREFERENCES:

Patterns to avoid:

MATERIAL PREFERENCES:

    Flooring:

    Cabinetry:

    Countertops:

    Walls:

LIFESTYLE:

    Casual?

    Informal?

    Formal?

    Elegant?

TASTE OF OCCUPANTS:

    Likes:

    Dislikes:

    Styles—the latest or what suits you?

FUNCTION OF SPACE/ACTIVITIES IN SPACE:

FAVORITE HOME DESIGN RESOURCES:

    Print magazines (and/or their Web sites):

    Design-focused Web Sites:

    Manufacturer's Web Sites:

    Television Shows/Movies:

FIGURE 2.2 A unified kitchen

Design by David McFadden, codesigner Debbie Larson; Past Basket Design, Geneva, IL
Photo by David McFadden

FIGURE 2.3 A unified bathroom
Design by Lynn David Monson, CKD, CBD, codesigner Sandy J. Monson; Monson Interior Design, Minneapolis, MN
Photo by Mark Ehlen/Ehlen Creative Communications

A Timeless Look

The second characteristic of good design is that it stands the test of time. Experienced designers tend to avoid fads and turn a skeptical eye on what is currently defined as trendy or fashionable. They concentrate on proven style and solid quality, which is based on the appropriateness and durability of the design solutions and products that the client wants incorporated in the room. When evaluating a proposed solution or material for a major element in the room, ask the question: "Will this be considered pleasing and beautiful five years from now?" If you think not, you may want to try a different, more neutral approach for these long-lasting areas, whether based on traditional, historical (see Figures 2.4 and 2.5) elements or more contemporary (see Figures 2.6 and 2.7) ones.

To add some punch to this cautious approach to design, specify bold patterns, colors, and/or accessories—or unique materials for surfaces that are easily changed over the life expectancy of the room (see Figures 2.8 and 2.9).

PERSONALIZING THE DESIGN

Successful designers strive to make the kitchens or bathrooms they create reflect the client's own interests and preferences rather than their own. It is not uncommon to see a series of projects created by a designer that all have the same or a very similar look to them. But the

FIGURE 2.4 Highly stylized traditional kitchen

Design by Peter Ross Salerno, CMKBD, codesigner Diane Durocher; Peter Salerno, Inc., Wyckoff, NJ
Photo by Peter Rymwid Architectural Photography

good, skilled, and creative professional designs each project so it is an individual, personal expression of the specific client.

To accomplish this, the designer should first spend time listening rather than talking. Interior design professionals call this the program phase of the design process. Quite simply, the first thing you must do is gather as much information as you can from the client. Using your own information-gathering system or the detailed survey form developed by the National Kitchen & Bath Association, conscientious designers ask a series of preplanned questions and take careful note of client answers in an organized fashion. Some specific types of questions to ask clients related directly to the aesthetics of the design as well as the style theme desired are included in Table 2.1 and can be adapted to suit each project.

During this information-gathering stage, it is not appropriate to be focused on solutions. Rather, it is time to learn what clients like and dislike about their existing room and what their dreams and hopes are for their new kitchen or bathroom. It is also important to establish the budget range for the project as well.

FIGURE 2.5 Highly stylized traditional bathroom
Design by Lori W. Carroll, NCIDQ/ASID; Lori Carroll & Associates, Tucson, AZ
Photo by William Lesch

The information gathered should be divided into four categories:

1. **General client information.** See Client Profile Survey Form, Table 2.1.
2. **Budget range for the project.** Knowing the financial limitations is as important as knowing clients' favorite colors.
3. **Time frame.** If deadlines exist for the completion of the project, this may restrict the extent of design or structural changes and proposed list of products.
4. **Who the key decision makers are.** Is an interior designer involved, or an architect or other key individuals who will be part of the decision-making process?

Design professionals often overlook the need to understand budget constraints as a key element of their practice. However, the best in the business get a good sense of what the budget is before they begin the planning process. Budgets affect design solutions and product choices.

Tips from the Pros: How to Talk about the Budget with Your Client

The first thing I do when interviewing a client in the showroom or beginning a presentation is to give them choices. I want them to feel that even though I am in control of the design, they're in control of the budget. I'm not just a salesperson trying to push the price as high as I can. A client said to me the other day, "Well, I do have a budget." I said, "Everybody has a budget, it's just some budgets are bigger than others." My clients know I respect their budget and my industry knowledge will help them invest their money wisely."

—Designer in Connecticut

We usually discuss the budget right from the beginning and make it clear we put it at the top of our list of "needs." Just as more storage in a kitchen or a particular type of counter surface in the bath is a "need," we tell our clients the budget should be at the top of that list as well.

—Designer in Georgia

I usually ask the client to give me an "investment" price rather than a "budget" price.

—Designer in Colorado

If we've selected a cabinet line, and the dollar amount for those cabinets isn't within the client's range, I show them alternative options, whether it's a less expensive door or a more modestly priced finish option. I try to show them ways to keep the same design but price it out for less.

—Designer in California

Questions to Ask the Client

Following the general information, you as the designer will need to ask specific questions about how the kitchen or bath is used. This is how you determine ways to personalize the space. For example, the kitchen designed strictly for adults who really do not cook at home allows far more latitude in product specifications than does a space that will be used by a busy family with three active teenagers or young children who cook day in and day out. And an infrequently used powder room is planned differently from a hall bathroom used by the entire family or a master bathroom used by one or two people.

In addition to asking specific questions about the kitchen and bath, pay close attention to how the room relates to adjacent spaces.

Here are some examples of some of the situations that might be encountered:

- **Is the kitchen part of a general great room in the public areas of the home?** If so, it must be integrated with these other living spaces.
- **Is the kitchen a walled-off separate space located between the living and formal dining rooms?** Continuity between the various rooms may not be as important to the homeowners.

FIGURE 2.6 A timeless design—kitchen
Design by Beverly Adams, CMKBD, Denver, CO

- **Is the kitchen next to a family room or a breakfast nook?** Such a room arrangement may let you combine the spaces into an open multipurpose area. When next to the family room, much more attention will be paid to the style details of this space because it must look like a living space as much as it does a kitchen.
- **Is the bathroom part of the master bedroom suite?** It then needs to be integrated with the bedroom space.
- **What fixture options are desired?** Space needs to be allocated to accommodate them and their use as well as considering plumbing and other structural and mechanical locations and considerations.

Product Specifications

Next, focus on specific products—do clients need a built-in combination microwave/convection/steam oven or a freestanding 60-inch professional range? Is a freestanding soaking tub their dream—or a spa-like jetted tub for two high on their priority list?

Noting all the client's preferences is a starting point—this is where you begin to personalize the space. At a later date, you may need to suggest alternatives to the homeowner. (See the *Kitchen & Bath Products and Materials* volume of the NKBA Professional Resource

FIGURE 2.7 A timeless design—bathroom
Design by Jamieson Simpson, CKD; Harrell Remodeling Inc., Mountain View, CA
Photo by Dean J. Birinyi

Library for suggestions.) The place to start is at the beginning: by listening more than talking.

Existing Construction

As the designer, take note of construction constraints that may affect the design recommendations, as well as architectural or mechanical elements of the space that must be considered as you create the aesthetic design solution. (See *Kitchen Planning, Bath Planning,* and *Kitchen & Bath Residential Construction and Systems* volumes of the NKBA Professional Resource Library for specific details.)

Design Information

The color and design specifics you gathered help you personalize space for each client.

A good time to share your portfolio (either digital or actual photographs) with prospective clients is as you begin asking color and design questions. By using perspectives of completed

FIGURE 2.8 A timeless look with punch—kitchen
Design by Jennifer Gilmer, CKD; Jennifer Gilmer Kitchen & Bath, Ltd., Chevy Chase, MD
Photo by Bob Narod Photography, LLC

kitchens/bathrooms or photographs of actual projects, you can show clients what different styles look like as well as examples of your work.

An excellent visual tool to help suggest and describe design solutions is an idea book of images: either a digital book from various design Web sites or images cut from magazines, divided by various themes and room layout possibilities. It is as important to find out what prospective clients don't like—colors, styles, or products—as it is to determine what they do like, so you can remove options from consideration. Often consumers have pictures, either hard copies or their own digital books, or some of both, that they have carefully collected over the years that reflect their wants and desires for the new room. Ask clients to show you the images they have collected. Look carefully at the pictures and ask clients, "What is it about this picture that you like and why? Is there anything you don't like?" Be sure to clarify between functional preferences and stylistic ones.

Document the Information Gathered

It is important for the designer to take good notes, making copies for client files as well. It is not unusual for designers to take digital photographs of the house exterior, the room under

FIGURE 2.9 A timeless look with punch—bathroom

Design by Barbara E. Murphy, CKD, CBD; Neil Kelly Design, Build & Remodeling, Lake Oswego, OR

discussion, and adjacent living spaces during the home survey appointment. This visual reference helps designers study the details of the client's home as the planning and personalization process begins.

Final Design Consideration

When you complete the client survey in this manner, you will have carefully noted and cataloged the project limitations, client needs and desires, and product requests. This helps you determine how to take the necessary centers of activity in the kitchen or bathroom and combine them so that they form a well-organized, functional room within the construction limitations and budget constraints of the project.

After you complete the conceptual space layout, you will use the intangible design guides tools of the design trade, the elements and principles of design, to create an aesthetically pleasing and unique project.

SUMMARY

This chapter discusses some of the basic steps of planning and creating a design for clients that is creative, personal, unique, and meets their functional and aesthetic needs. Also included are some suggested questions to pose to clients about any desired theme or style specific to the kitchen and bathroom.

REVIEW QUESTIONS

1. What specific information needs to be gathered from the client to begin a design project? (See "Personalizing the Design" pages 18–20, and "Questions to Ask the Client" pages 19–20)

2. Describe how a designer can create a personalized and unique space for the client. (See "Personalizing the Design" pages 18–20)

3. Describe what design skills are, and explain how to assist clients in developing their own design style. (See "Developing Design Style" pages 14–15)

4. Describe how one develops creativity and applies it to design solutions. (See "Creativity: Is It a Natural Gift, or Can It Be Learned?" page 15)

Elements of Design

Often overlooked in the design of kitchens and bathrooms is the conscious consideration, application, and use of the elements and principles of design. Typically, designers think of them as applicable only to the primary living/social and private spaces of the home. However, as the kitchen and bathroom spaces or areas have become more integrated into these living and private spaces, their application and use have increased in consideration and importance. An understanding of the elements and principles of design assists the designer in finding the best, most functional, and often a unique solution for a particular space. The elements are the designer's tools, concrete and quantifiable. The principles are the theory or guidelines that direct designers in the use of those tools, applying the elements appropriately in their designs of spaces. The designer needs to be familiar with the elements, or tools, and then use them to follow the design principles to create a total environment. The design principles are discussed in chapter 4. The elements and principles included in the discussion in this chapter and in Chapter 4 are those most often included and discussed in interior design overview texts. Not everyone agrees. Likewise, most present the design elements prior to the principles, which is how they are usually taught.

The eight elements of design are:

1. Line   **5.** Form
2. Shape   **6.** Texture
3. Pattern   **7.** Color
4. Space   **8.** Light

Learning Objective 1: Name and define the elements of design.

Learning Objective 2: Cite an example of the use of each of the design elements in kitchens and bathrooms.

Learning Objective 3: Describe the effect on a kitchen and bathroom space of the use of different kinds of lines.

Learning Objective 4: Describe some of the effects of color in kitchens and bathrooms.

Learning Objective 5: Describe some of the effects of light that need to be considered in kitchens and bathrooms.

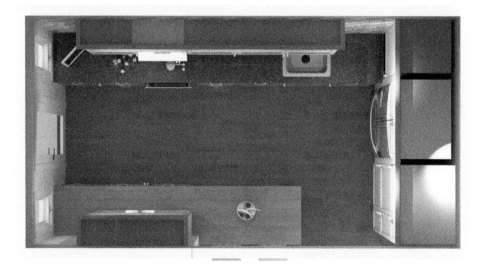

FIGURE 3.1 Kitchen featuring predominantly horizontal lines

Design by Tim Scott, codesigners Erica Esterorth, CKD, NCIDQ and Sheena Hammond, XTC Design Inc., Toronto, ON
Arnal Photography

LINE

A line is created by the connection between two points, the simplest of elements. Line can evoke an emotional response and have the ability to stretch or shrink space visually. Joining several lines together creates shapes. The section "Shape" in this chapter includes specific examples and illustrations of different shapes lines create that can be found in kitchens and bathrooms.

A design rarely features just one type of line. Several types of lines are used in most spaces. However, generally one type of line predominates and contributes to the overall feeling of the space. Examples of such combinations follow as each type of line and shape is discussed.

Horizontal Line

The horizontal line is the most stable of all line forms. The eye travels along the horizontal line, visually widening the area or object viewed. Horizontal lines usually invoke a feeling of calm and suggest rest, relaxation, and informality. When horizontal lines are the dominant lines in a room, they can help to visually expand and widen the space. Often this is a consideration in small kitchens and bathrooms, such as those that are narrow, or those with high ceilings. Wide horizontal lines that contrast strongly with background surfaces divide the overall elevation into alternating segments. Such a horizontal division works well to visually readjust the ceiling height in a room by lowering it, then concentrating on expanding the feeling of greater width and space (see Figures 3.1 and 3.2).

Vertical Line

A vertical line carries the eye upward and adds visual height to the space. It expresses forcefulness and can have a formal, austere feeling. Some viewers interpret the vertical line as being rigid. Vertical line can be created by a patterned surface, by contrasting colors of the same material, or by combining dissimilar materials in a predominantly vertical fashion along one or more elevations of the room.

Be aware that the width of the line, the space between the lines, and the contrast between the finish or color of the line and adjacent spaces all affect the impact of vertical lines. Narrow pinstripe lines usually feel softer than strong, wide bands of widely contrasting colors. Closely spaced, thin vertical lines can visually widen a room as the eye follows them, as well as add height often necessary when the ceiling is a lower than desired height. Figures 3.3 and 3.4 show the use of vertical lines to visually add height and width to these kitchen and bathroom spaces.

Curved Line

The infinite variety of curved lines makes them useful in expressing both contemporary and traditional movements and feelings. A full, tightly wound curve can encourage activity as the eye follows it, appropriate in active contemporary kitchen and bathroom spaces. A soft gentle, undulating curve, especially in the horizontal direction, can suggest refinement and restfulness, a characteristic of more formal, traditional rooms. Curves that are asymmetrical and free-formed can also add a bit of whimsy to a space.

Curved lines generally have a feminine feeling and usually soften a space. They work well in both kitchen and bathroom environments, which are often made up of predominantly straight, hard-edged and hard-textured surfaces. A kitchen mantel or vent hood area may be accentuated with a curved apron panel. Introducing a curved line in the counter surface can dramatically soften island or peninsula ends. In Figure 3.5, curves add movement and whimsy to this contemporary kitchen yet are also functional as door and drawer hardware. In the bathroom, adding a curved cabinet front in the vanity unit or curving the counter surface over such a unit softens the look (see Figure 3.6).

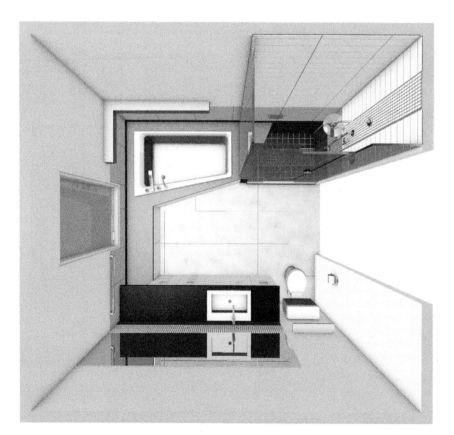

FIGURE 3.2 Bathroom featuring predominantly horizontal lines

Design by Jan E. Regis, CMKBD, Binns Kitchen + Bath Design, Pickering, ON
Photo by Tim McClean

FIGURE 3.3 Kitchen featuring predominantly vertical lines
Design by Rose Marie Carr, Kitchens by Rose, Ramsey, NJ
Photo by Peter Rymid Architectural Photographer

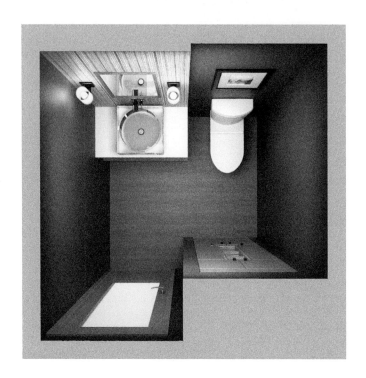

FIGURE 3.4 Bathroom featuring predominantly vertical lines

Design by John Mills Davies, CGBP, Marrokal Design & Remodeling, San Diego, CA

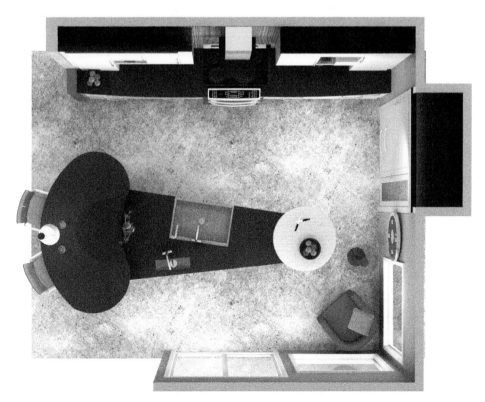

FIGURE 3.5 Kitchen featuring curved lines

Design by Rhonda Knoche, CMKBD, Rhonda Knoche Design, Portland, OR Photo by Cabin 4D Images

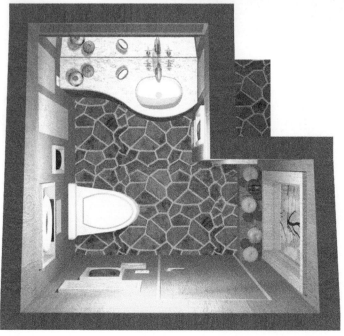

FIGURE 3.6 Bathroom featuring curved lines

Design by Elina Katsioula-Beall, CKD, Dewitt Designer Kitchens, Pasadena, CA
Photo by Suki Medencevic

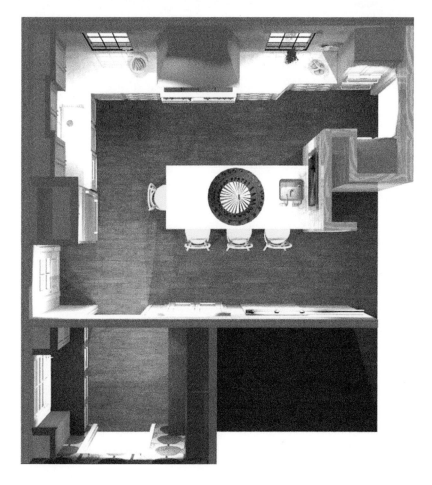

FIGURE 3.7 Kitchen featuring diagonal lines

Design by Karen Swanson, New England Design Works, Manchester, MA
Photo by Evan White

Diagonal Line

The diagonal line is often dramatic. It forces the eye in either a predominantly horizontal or vertical direction, or both if zigzagged, as in a chevron or herringbone configuration. A diagonal line implies action and movement. It has an energetic, vibrant feeling that encourages activity, though it sometimes can be disconcerting or disturbing, depending on the angle and any contrast, especially color contrast. Much like vertical lines, diagonal lines that don't contrast strongly with the background are easier to view in a small, confined space than are large, contrasting diagonal lines. However, strong contrasts of diagonal lines do draw attention and can become a focal point in the room.

For example, a kitchen may feature a dramatic angled line in the vent hood located above the cooking center. Such a line can contrast or blend, depending on color, with the backsplash or other wall material that is repeated in a different way such as the subtle chevron-inspired wallpaper in Figure 3.7. Another interesting way to use an angled line is to install decorative ceramic or stone tiles in a zig-zag chevron pattern in contrasting colors along the sink backsplash (see Figure 3.8) or on the diagonal in a shower area in the bathroom when the ceiling height changes, giving an impression of larger space (see Figure 3.9).

Some kitchens are very small, and most bathrooms are limited in space, so the impact of diagonal lines can either visually expand the space or be overpowering. Think about the overall impact of the lines as the arrangement of cabinetry, accessories, surface treatments, and walls within the bathroom or small kitchen develops by visualizing the space with detailed elevations or a perspective, in addition to the floor plan.

FIGURE 3.8 Backsplash featuring diagonal lines
Courtesy of Kohler Company

FIGURE 3.9 Bathroom featuring diagonal lines

Design by Jon Crabtree, Inspired Spaces, Minneapolis, MN
Photo by SP Photo Design

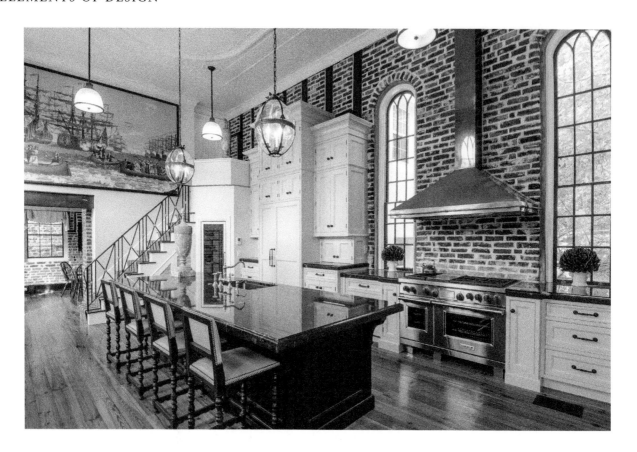

FIGURE 3.10 Combining lines in a kitchen

Design by Bryan Reiss, CMKBD, codesigners Susanna Caongor and Diane Murphy, Distinctive Design, Mt. Pleasant, SC
Photo by John D. Smoak III

Combining Lines

Lines can be used to create a space that is restful or active, peaceful or busy. Too much of any one type of line may be visually uninteresting; however, one type should dominate with other lines used in lesser, unequal amounts. Too many contrasting or too equal amounts of lines cause visual confusion and can shrink the perception of space, especially in a small room. It is probably wise to err on the conservative side when arranging lines within a kitchen or bathroom. A simple room always can be enhanced with accents and accessories later. It's more difficult to tone down an overdone room. The kitchen in Figure 3.10 illustrates this concept: Vertical lines dominate—cabinetry, vent stack, tall, narrow windows, and lighting fixtures, drawing the eye upward to emphasize the high ceiling, accentuating the generous size of the room. Subordinate to that are horizontal lines in the brick, large pieces of art, and contrasting countertop, then diagonal lines with the range hood and stair case railing, and finally, the curved light fixtures in the smallest amount. The same holds true for the bathroom in Figure 3.11: Vertical lines dominate with the windows, vanity light fixtures, and walls, then horizontal lines with the cabinetry and contrasting window framing; diagonal lines with the ceiling and floor tile layout to visually widen the room; and finally, the curves of the tub and vanity bowls add a subtle softness.

FIGURE 3.11 Combining lines in a bathroom

Design by Lilley E. Yee, CMKBD CID, ASID, Lilley Yee Interiors, San Mateo, CA
Photography Copyright Dean J. Birinyi, ASMP

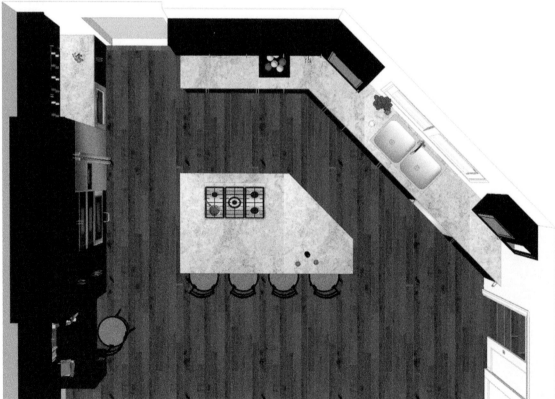

FIGURE 3.12 Kitchen designed with predominantly rectangular shapes

Design by Sanchali Srivastava, CKD, CID, San Interior Design, San Jose, CA
Photo by Mark Pinkerton

SHAPE

Line is the simplest element of a shape; each shape is a two-dimensional configuration of two or more lines linked together. Therefore, connected lines make up shapes, which can be used to change the way the space is perceived. The simplest shapes used in design are rectangular, square, diagonal or angles, triangular and curved.

Rectangular Shape

Rectangles are two-dimensional shapes formed by connecting four lines of two different lengths together, forming ninety-degree angles. Because of their regular and vertical or horizontal nature, rectangles are easy shapes for most people to relate to. Rectangles are usually of varying sizes to add interest and are used in cabinetry doors and drawers, as well as the appliances, chair backs, and flooring, as seen in Figure 3.12 and the mirror along with cabinetry in Figure 3.13.

Square Shape

In a square, all sides are equal. There is little movement because of the sameness and regularity and this can lead to an uninteresting room, especially if there are too many square shapes of the same size. An effective use of square shapes in a kitchen is shown in Figure 3.14 in the square glass cabinet inserts combined to form rectangles. Another effective use is shown with the repeating wall tile in the bathroom in Figure 3.15.

Diagonal or Angled Shape

Diagonal or angled shapes imply movement and activity and are the least stable shapes. The direction of the slant draws the eye along its path and gives this impression of movement. These shapes are strong and can dominate the design and visually expand or make better use of a narrow space. In Figure 3.16 the diagonal shape of the peninsula allows for it to be larger and the corner cabinet next to the window visually wider as well as making better use of the space in this kitchen. In Figure 3.17 the angle of the shower enclosure and the diagonal placement of the tub allow for both to be included without sacrificing much-needed floor space. When an angled shape has more than four or five sides, it can begin to take on the characteristics of a circle as the number of sides is increased.

Triangular Shape

The triangle is the most stable of the angled shapes when the base is at the bottom of the elevation or shape. A triangle is less stable when the narrowest point is at the bottom. The range vent hood shown in Figure 3.18 conveys this feeling of a stable triangular shape. In Figure 3.19, the inverted triangular shape of the vessel sinks becomes more stable by eliminating the point at the bottom.

Curved or Circular Shapes

A curve visually expands a space by allowing the eye to move continuously throughout its length. A curved shape often dominates over a square or a rectangular one because of the movement created. The eye naturally follows around the arcs and the complete circle, as opposed to focusing on each separate wall or right angle of a square or a rectangle. The counters and peninsula in Figure 3.20 draw the eye all around the space, moving from one area to another, giving the feeling of greater space. Likewise, the curved counters and shelving in Figure 3.21 keep the eye moving around a relatively small space, visually widening it as well.

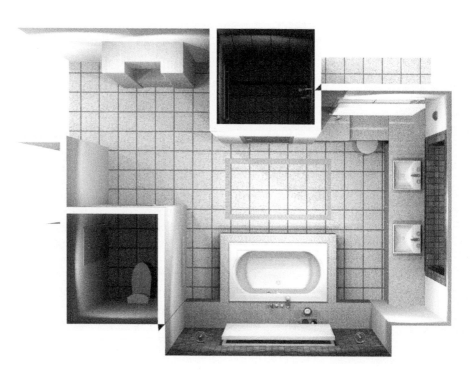

FIGURE 3.13 Bathroom designed with predominantly rectangular shapes

Design by Elina Katsioula-Beall, CKD, Dewitt Designer Kitchens, Pasadena, CA
Photo by Suki Mendencevic

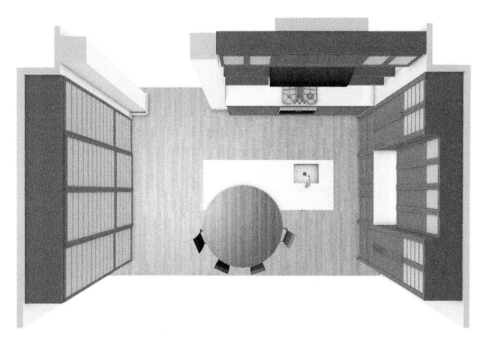

FIGURE 3.14 Kitchen designed with square shapes

Design by Jennifer L. Gilmer, CKD, Jennifer Gilmer Kitchen & Bath, Ltd., Chevy Chase, MD
Bob Narod Photography, LLC

FIGURE 3.15 Bathroom designed with square shapes

Design by Michael Bright, codesigners Sonya Faulhaber and John Sarkesian, Bright Wood Works, Inc., St. Petersburg, FL
Photo by baptiephoto.com

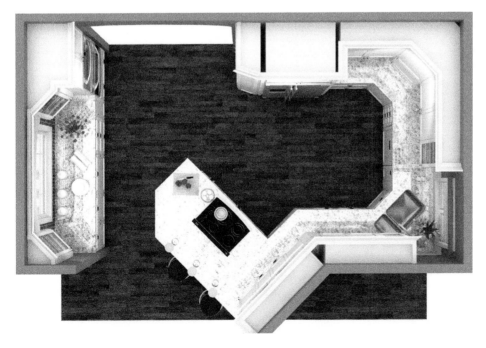

FIGURE 3.16 Kitchen designed with diagonal and angled shapes

Design by Angela Victoria Rasmussen, House 2 Home Design & Build, San Jose, CA
Dean J. Birinyi Photography

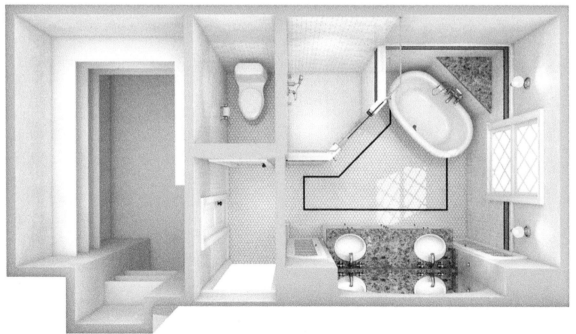

FIGURE 3.17 Bathroom designed with diagonal and angled shapes

Design by Adrienne Dorig Leland, CKD, Dorig Designs, Claremont, CA Photo by Ken B. Henry

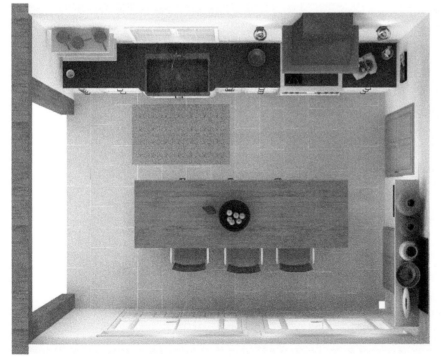

FIGURE 3.18 Kitchen designed with triangular shapes

Design by Richard Ourso, CKD, CAPS, codesigners Vickie Mire, CKD, CAPS, and Michelle Livings, AKBD, CAPS, LEED, Ourso Designs, Baton Rouge, LA
Photo by Chipper Hatter

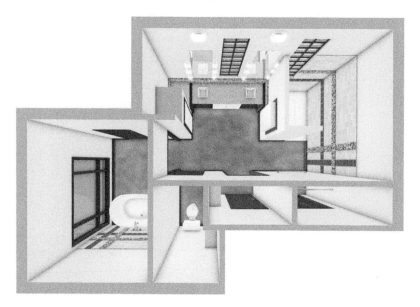

FIGURE 3.19 Bathroom designed with triangular shapes

Design by Brian M. Johnson, AIA,
Collaborative Design Architects,
Billings, MT
Photo by Phil Bell

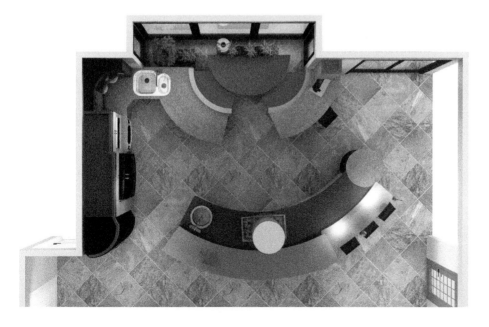

FIGURE 3.20 Kitchen designed with curved and circular shapes

Design by Glen Prairie, CKD, codesigner Celeste Pilon; Total Living Concepts, Barrie, ON Barrer Photography

FIGURE 3.21 Bathroom designed with curved and circular shapes

Design by Lori W. Carroll, NCIDQ\ ASID, codesigner Mary Roles, Lori Carroll & Associates, Tucson, AZ Jon Mancuso Photography

FIGURE 3.22 Kitchen with structural pattern

Design by Roger W. Zierman, Partners 4 Design, Minneapolis, MN
Gilberson Photography

IDENTIFYING PATTERN PREFERENCES

After becoming familiar with various lines and shapes, designers combine them into patterns that support the design theme. Patterns are made up of elements of design: notably lines and shapes. A "pattern" can be defined as something the eye follows. It is the arrangement of motifs or designs (shapes) in either a repetitive or a varied order. Design patterns are also classified in five broad categories. Designers who can identify the client's pattern preference will then find the most appropriate direction to follow in product and material recommendations.

The five broad categories are:

1. Structural
2. Naturalistic
3. Stylized
4. Geometric
5. Abstract

All of these categories offer possibilities in keeping with both the style and the mood of different motifs. Following are a series of kitchens and bathrooms that include examples of these various pattern categories.

Structural Pattern

Structural pattern allows the intrinsic structure and material of the product or space to determine the form of the design, generally without any applied ornamentation. Enrichment and pattern come from the material along with the structural design of the object. For example, the grain in woods, cabinetry, or floors; the veins and coloration in slate; the specks in granite or stonelike surface materials without additional adornment all fall into the category of structural pattern. Clients who prefer a simple, uncluttered, and natural presentation of materials as well as contemporary design styles often choose predominantly structural design. In Figures 3.22 and 3.23 the shape of the cabinetry and fixtures, as well as the color and textures of the materials are examples of structural pattern—no other ornamentation was applied.

Naturalistic Pattern

Naturalistic pattern represents subject matter drawn from nature, such as flowers, leaves, fruits, animals, and landscapes. The motif is as realistic as possible, so these natural elements are readily identifiable. The colors frequently are related to those found in nature. Such designs are typically seen in decorative ceramic tiles, custom-painted scenic murals, wallpaper patterns or borders, and fabrics designed and selected for the kitchen or bathroom space. These patterns lend themselves to several types of rooms, including formal and informal, traditional, eclectic, and contemporary rooms. In Figure 3.24 the hand-painted wall tiles above the cooktop form a realistic plant arrangement image, and in Figure 3.25 the hand-painted fish and water plant images on the floor of this bathroom give one the feeling of them actually being there.

Stylized Pattern

Stylized pattern is drawn from recognized natural sources, but the pattern makes no pretense at actually representing a specific object or source. The themes used can be simplified, exaggerated, rearranged, or distorted to achieve the purposes of the design. A stencil pattern on the wall in a Pennsylvania farmhouse kitchen is an example of a stylized pattern. Such patterns are also often selected for fabric, wallpaper, or border choices. Many ceramic tile decorative patterns feature a stylized motif, as seen above the cooktop in Figure 3.26 and the wall tile pattern above the bathtub in Figure 3.27.

FIGURE 3.23 Bathroom with structural pattern

Design by Ines Hanl, codesigner Kimberly Lewis Manning, The Sky is the Limit Design, Victoria, BC
Works Photography

FIGURE 3.24 Kitchen with naturalistic pattern

Design by Jane Lockhart, Jane Lockhart Interior Design, Toronto, ON
Photo by Brandon Barre

FIGURE 3.25 Bathroom with naturalistic pattern

Design by Tess Giuliani, CKD, Tess Giuliani Designs, Inc., Ridgewood, NJ Peter Rymwid Architectural Photography

FIGURE 3.26 Kitchen with stylized pattern

Design by Peter Ross Salerno, CMKBD, codesigners Marsha Thornhill and Kimberly Hill, CKD, CBD, Peter Salerno Inc., Wyckoff, NJ Peter Rymwid Architectural Photography

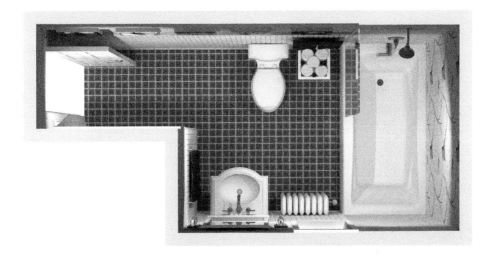

FIGURE 3.27 Bathroom with stylized pattern

Design by Cindy McClure, CKD, MCR, CGP, codesigner DC Design House, Grossmueller's Design Consultants, Washington, DC Photo by John Tsantes

FIGURE 3.28 Kitchen with geometric pattern

Design by Wendy F. Johnson, CKD, CBD, Design for Living, Manchester Village, VT
Photo by Dennis Martin

Geometric Pattern

A geometric pattern follows mathematically derived and predictable formulas. Circles, triangles, rectangles, stripes, plaids, polka dots, and lacy patterns are all based on geometric forms. This type of pattern works well when colors or shapes of the same naturalistic materials are also combined. Eclectic and modern kitchens and bathrooms, which typically have little applied ornamentation, often showcase geometric patterns, as seen in the floor pattern in Figure 3.28 and the wall mosaic in Figure 3.29.

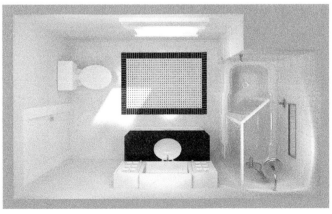

FIGURE 3.29 Bathroom with geometric pattern

Design by Victoria Shaw, Binns Kitchen + Bath Design, Pickering, ON
Photo by Tim McClean Photography

Abstract Pattern

An abstract pattern typically is based on some geometric form but introduces an element of impressionism and artistic freedom, deviating from the original shape. The shapes and patterns are less regular, rigid, and formal than the traditional concept of geometric design and usually are not recognizable as any particular object or design. Such a pattern may work well along the backsplash, as part of a countertop, or for a lighting fixture as seen in the kitchen in Figure 3.30. Bathrooms may feature an abstract pattern design within the vanity, sink fixture, or as a wall treatment (see Figure 3.31).

Combining Patterns

It is not unusual in today's interior design to combine several patterns in one space. Many of these combinations are extremely successful while others can seem incompatible. This potential incompatibility has been a source of insecurity for both designers and clients, especially when the influence of any current fashion and design trends adds to the confusion. There have been

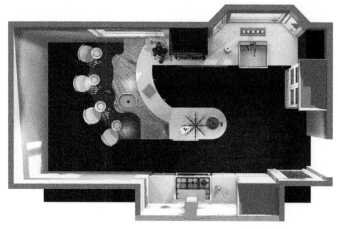

FIGURE 3.30 Kitchen with abstract pattern

Design by Elina Katsioula-Beall, CKD, Dewitt Designer Kitchens, Pasadena, CA
Photo by Suki Medencevic

FIGURE 3.31 Bathroom with abstract pattern
*Design by Erica Westeroth, CKD, codesigner Tim Scott; XTC Design Incorporated, Toronto, ON
Photo by Donna Griffith Photography*

periods in history when many patterns, particularly florals or geometrics, were used together everywhere, and other times when little or no pattern was used. To combine several patterns together successfully, the designer needs to consider these guiding principles:

- **Utilize color continuity among the different patterns to tie them together.** This creates unity among them, generally a single color or two common to all the patterns. To add interest and variety, vary the value, intensity, and amounts of color used. Using a larger amount of one color with lesser amounts of others also helps achieve unity.
- **Ensure there is style or theme consistency among patterns used.** It doesn't matter if the patterns are traditional, contemporary, classical, country, formal, or informal: This is a guiding principle.
- **Different types of patterns used together create interest and can avoid conflict.** Mix geometric with stylized or naturalistic, abstract with stylized, for example.
- **Vary the size and scale of the patterns.** Combine large with medium and or small. Size can give one pattern more importance than others.
- **Vary the intensity of patterns.** Use some that are bold and dominant, others that are less intense or subdued, so as not to compete with one another for attention.
- **Include both intricate and subtle, simpler patterns.** This provides contrast and interest.
- **Different amounts of pattern are important.** Usually utilize an odd number, which helps avoid having equal amounts. Select one pattern to dominate and serve as the reference point for all the patterns in the space, then use lesser amounts of the others.
- **Utilize areas of solids, textures, and neutrals.** These areas are important to separate patterns and avoid the busy look of too many patterns right next to each other.

The kitchen in Figure 3.32 illustrates the appropriate application of combining multiple patterns in the area behind the range. The two different tile patterns are similar in color but separated by the solid space of the frames.

FIGURE 3.32 Kitchen using multiple patterns

Design by Ines Hanl, codesigner Kimberly Lewis Mannig, The Sky is the Limit, Victoria, BC
Photo by Jo-Ann Richards, Works Photography

SPACE

Space is created by adding walls, enclosing the floor and ceiling of the home, and is the three-dimensional area creating rooms. The overall space of the room, with its doors and windows, ceiling height, walls, and millwork, is the envelope the designer works within. It is the space people move around in and that objects occupy. It can be either closed (with the room having four walls and a door) or open and be part of another space or room. It can be large or small and a variety of shapes. Most residential rooms, including kitchens and bathrooms, however, tend to be some variation of the rectangle, although irregular shapes, such as curves or angles, are not uncommon particularly if they open into an adjacent space.

A kitchen or bathroom space is defined by the objects or forms that occupy the area within the room. The relationship of these parts to the total arrangement of the room becomes the "space." To successfully plan kitchens or bathrooms, it is critical to understand the relationship between the individual form of an object and the overall space (or room) it occupies.

FIGURE 3.33 Kitchen with a pyramid form. The center cabinet over the sink is raised above the adjacent wall units, creating a pyramid shape.
Design by Pietro Giorgi, Sr., CMKBD and Ellen Cheever, CMKBD, ASID, Giorgi Kitchens and Designs, Wilmington, DE
Photo by McClain Imagery

FORM

The form of an object is determined by its structure, size, apparent weight, and ornamentation. Therefore, form is not just the physical shape of the object. Rather, it is determined by the overall structure of the shape and the relationship of that shape with others adjacent to it.

Remember: If the form (visual size) of an object is minimized so it blends with the surrounding space, the form (visual size) of the entire room grows in visual importance. That is why an item in a room seems larger if emphasis is placed on it by contrasting it with adjacent or adjoining objects. A room almost always appears smaller if there are numerous contrasting items in it.

One way designers emphasize specific forms in a room is to contrast the heights of vertical elements throughout the space. This can be accomplished in three ways.

1. **Create a pyramid.** With this approach, the tallest vertical element is in the center and adjacent elements grow smaller in descending order, as seen with the cabinetry arrangement over the sinks in Figures 3.33 and 3.34.
2. **Create an "H" form.** Taller elements are placed at each end of a lower form, a run of cabinets or a window, as examples. This forms a symmetrically balanced "H" shape on the wall elevation. Cabinets resting on the countertop or extending to the ceiling may accomplish this. Or use both of these approaches combined along one elevation, as seen in Figures 3.35 and 3.36.
3. **Create a step ladder.** The tallest element appears at one or both ends of the wall elevation, with all other elements growing progressively smaller (see Figure 3.37).

FIGURE 3.34 Bathroom with a pyramid form. The center cabinet is raised above the adjacent tile back splashes, creating a pyramid shape.
Design by Ines Hanl, codesigner Kimberly Lewis Manning, The Sky is the Limit Design, Victoria, BC
Photo by Works Photography

FIGURE 3.35 Kitchen with an H form. By dropping the wall cabinets suspended between the two tall built-in appliance elements, an H shape is created.

Design by Judy Adams Hunt, Sarasota, FL

FIGURE 3.36 Bathroom with an H form. The lower window between the taller wall cabinets and tile pattern creates the H shape.

Design by Angela Rasmussen, codesigner Taryne Meyer, House 2 Home Design Build, San Jose, CA
Photograph Copyright Dean J. Birinyi, ASMP

FIGURE 3.37 Create a stepladder-form kitchen. The cabinetry over the sink creates a stepladder or staircase form on each side within the design.
Design by Gerard Ciccarello, CMKBD, Covenant Kitchens & Baths, Inc., Westbrook, CT
Photo by Jim Flora Studio, LLC

TEXTURE

Texture is defined as the roughness or smoothness of a surface, and it is noted either visually or by touch. There are two types of texture. The first is the actual texture, or the tactile quality of a surface: the sensation one feels when touching the surface. Is it smooth, rough, jagged, soft, hard, cold, clearly defined, or subtle?

Second is the visual texture. The visual quality of an object allows the eye to feel the surface rather than with the fingers.

Just as the other elements of design trigger emotional responses, so do textures.

- Rough, course textures tend to have a rugged, sturdy quality, particularly when they dominate a space. They imply informality, a naturalistic, usually more casual asymmetrical arrangement, as seen in Figures 3.38 and 3.39, where the rough textures of the wall materials dominate.
- Fine, smooth, and shiny textures tend to suggest formality and elegance and a traditional or sophisticated contemporary, look. They may also imply a hard, cold feeling within the room (see Figure 3.40 and 3.41) when they dominate the space.

FIGURE 3.38 Guest house entertainment area with rough textures

Design by Holly Rickert, codesigner Julia Kleyman, Ulrich, Inc., Ridgewood, NJ
Peter Rymwid Architectural Photography

FIGURE 3.39 Bathroom with rough textures

Design by Lori W. Carroll, codesigner Mary Roles, Lori Carroll & Associates, Tucson, AZ
Photo by Jon Mancuso

Remember: Consider the texture of the various surfaces as you and your client select them.

- As a general rule, casual, country, and more masculine environments work best with strongly defined, rough-textured surfaces.
- Soft, gentle textures generally support formal, delicate, and feminine environments.
- Classically traditional rooms usually include a majority of smooth surfaces and soft, curved shapes.
- Contemporary modern rooms work well with smooth surfaces and strong textures (both rough and smooth) combined.

Combining various textures or massing one texture throughout the space is an effective way to have the room's design focus on the nature of the texture. This focus will appeal to clients who appreciate the beauty of natural materials: wood, stones, granite, ceramic, and heavy stucco wall surfaces. It is not unusual to combine various textures in a space, as seen in Figures 3.42 and 3.43. Typically, one will dominate.

COLOR

Because color appeals directly to emotions, it is a fascinating and powerful tool for the designer to work with. An explanation of some of the technical details of color follows. As the elements of color and light are closely tied together, each influencing the other, a brief discussion of light follows this section.

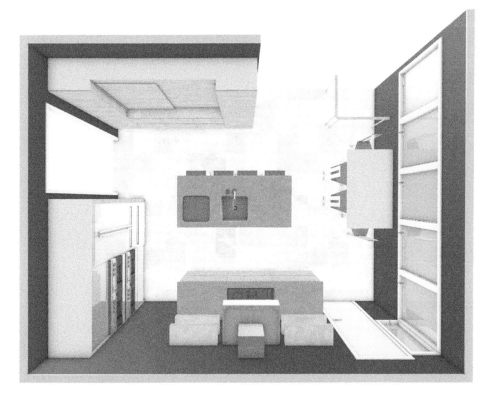

FIGURE 3.40 Kitchen with smooth textures

Design by Richard J. Farrell, Binns Kitchen + Bath Design, Pickering, ON Photo by Tim McClean

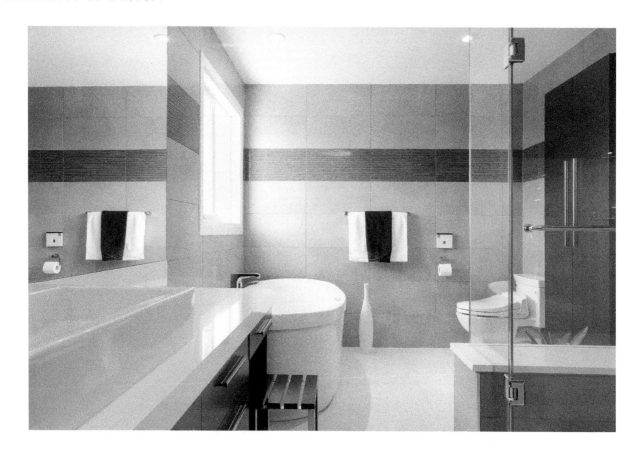

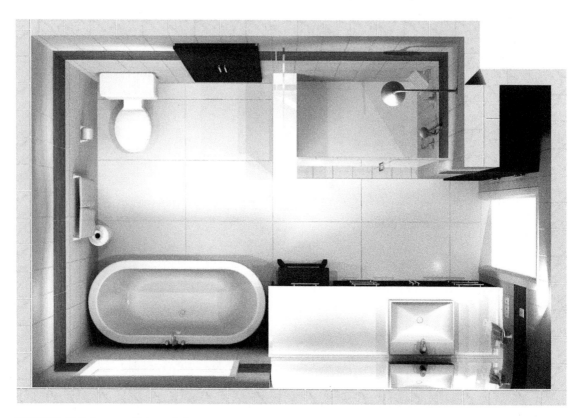

FIGURE 3.41 Bathroom with smooth textures

Design by Anastasia Rentzos, CKD, CBD, Andros Kitchen & Bath Designs, Mississauga, ON
Photo by Averill Lehan

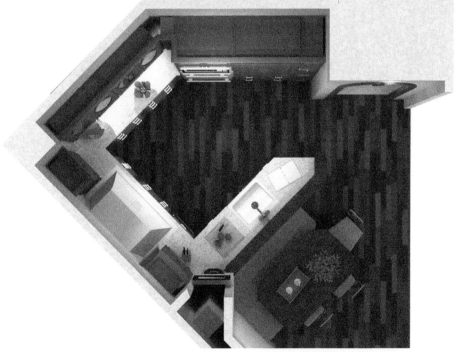

FIGURE 3.42 Kitchen combining smooth and rough textures

Design by Tracey Scalzo, CMKBD, Eurotech Cabinetry, Inc., Sarasota, FL Photo by Tom Harper Photography

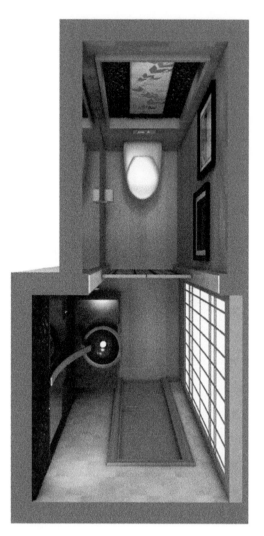

FIGURE 3.43 Bathroom combining smooth and rough textures

Design by Elina Katsioula-Beall, CKD, Dewitt Designer Kitchens, Inc., Pasadena, CA
Photo by Suki Medencevic

To become a more astute color specialist, increase your color sensitivity by paying particular attention to colors that surround you every day. Look at magazine advertisements. Study the sets in a television program or movie you are viewing. Pay attention to the colors used in store window displays. Collect photo examples, from design-oriented blogs and web sites and in print, of a variety of color schemes and uses of color. As your comfort level about color matures, your inhibitions about following the guidelines and rules of combining colors will begin to disappear and you will gain a freer approach to color expressions.

Hue

Colors are visible when light passes through a prism. The technical name given to a color as it is reflected through a prism is "hue." Hue is that attribute of a color by which we distinguish red from green, blue from yellow, and so on.

When a band of visible light is bent into a circle, a color wheel is created. Traditionally color wheels are shown with yellow at the top, but as long as the colors are correctly arranged, there is no absolute top or bottom to the wheel. The true value and intensity of each hue, as seen in nature, is reflected on the color wheel.

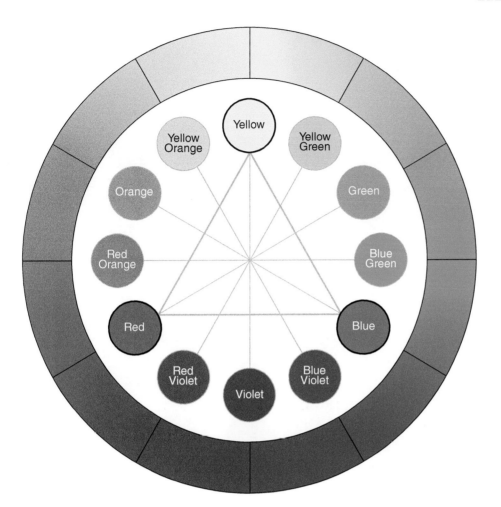

FIGURE 3.44 Color wheel

Objects in a room exhibit a particular color because of the selective nature by which their surfaces reflect and absorb light. As light strikes the colored surface, certain wavelengths are reflected to a greater extent than others. This reflected color determines what we see. White surfaces reflect all wavelengths equally and absorb little energy. Black surfaces absorb all wavelengths; therefore, we see the virtual absence of color.

Color Categories

The twelve principle hues (or colors) on the standard color wheel are divided into three categories: primary, secondary, and tertiary colors (see Figure 3.44).

Consider the color wheel with 12 equally spaced hues divided as follows (see Figure 3.45):

Primary hues. These are the colors from which all others are created. The primary colors are red, yellow, and blue. They are spaced at equal distances from one another on the color wheel.

Secondary hues. When two primary hues are combined the result is a secondary hue. Therefore, they are equally spaced between the primaries. Yellow and blue create green. Blue and red create violet. Red and yellow create orange.

Tertiary hues. Tertiary, or intermediate, colors are formed by combining adjacent primary and secondary colors. They are usually named with the primary color first, followed by the secondary color. Tertiary hues are yellow-green, blue-green, blue-violet, red-violet, red-orange, and yellow-orange.

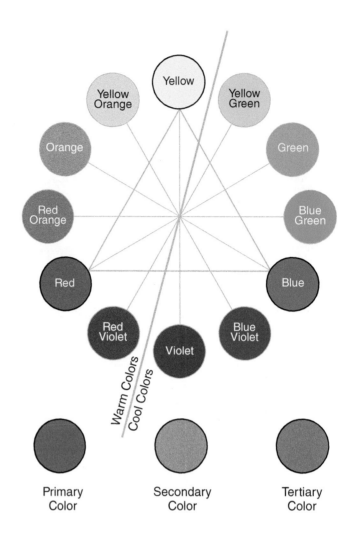

FIGURE 3.45 Three categories of hues on the color wheel

Color Attributes

Colors advance or recede. They are warm or cool. They are light or dark. They are bright or dull. In a traditional color wheel (12 hues, with yellow at the top) the colors on the left (in the red-through-yellow spectrum) are advancing, stimulating, warm colors. Colors on the right (in the blue, green, and violet collection) are receding, calming, and cool. When presented, the three attributes of color form a three-dimensional color wheel, as created and depicted by the noted colorist Albert Munsell (see Figure 3.46).

Color Intensity (Chroma)

Intensity (chroma) is the degree of departure of a color from the neutral or pure color of the same value. Colors of low intensity are sometimes called weak, while those of high intensity are said to be highly saturated, strong, or vivid.

When the intensity of a color is dull or grayed, it is identified as a tone. For example, burgundy is a tone of red. A bright color is usually identified as a pure color. A color called Christmas red is an example of a bright, pure red. The color's intensity is affected by the addition of its complement (the color directly opposite it on the color wheel) or by the addition of the neutral gray. Figure 3.47 illustrates the chroma scale for the color yellow.

FIGURE 3.46 Three-dimensional color wheel reflecting each hue's chroma and value

Color Value

The lightness or darkness of a color is referred to as its *value*. White is the highest value and black the lowest. Mixing white with the pure hue of a color, called a tint, produces a high value of a color. Pink is a tint of red. Mixing black with the hue produces a low value of a color, which is called a shade. A deep colonial red is an example of a shade of red. Figure 3.48 shows a value scale for red.

Color Schemes

Designers often assist clients in developing color schemes that appeal to them. Some specific color harmonies typically used in interiors can be categorized as shown and serve as a guide:

- Monochromatic
- Warm analogous
- Cool analogous
- Triad
- Complementary
- Neutral (achromatic)

FIGURE 3.47 Chroma scale for the color yellow

Monochromatic Scheme

A color scheme in which several different shades, tints, or tones of a single color are used is a monochromatic color scheme. In order to relieve any monotony that might occur, the scheme may use black, gray, white, or off white in addition to a variety of textures or patterns. Figure 3.49 is an example of a monochromatic kitchen color scheme that uses different values of yellow green on the walls with accents of beige and black. The monochromatic bathroom in Figure 3.50 uses the different values of blue in the mosaic tile wall, creating a focal point, and is offset with gray, white, and neutral wood tones.

Warm and Cool Analogous Schemes

A scheme in which several colors adjacent to one another on the color wheel are used together is called an analogous color scheme. One color generally dominates in this scheme. The colors used may vary in value and intensity. Depending on the colors selected, the overall scheme is generally either predominantly warm or cool. The kitchen in Figure 3.51 uses the warm analogous colors of yellow, yellow green in the wall and window

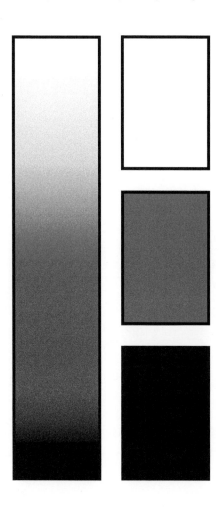

FIGURE 3.48 Value scale for red

FIGURE 3.49 Kitchen with a monochromatic color scheme

Design by Dana Jones, CKD, The Kitchen Consultant, Long Beach, CA Armen Asadorian Photography

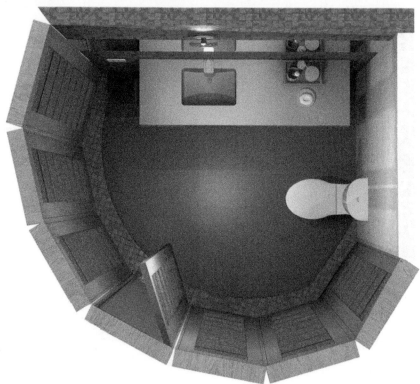

FIGURE 3.50 Bathroom with a monochromatic color scheme

Design by Gina Bon, CKD, CBD, Airoom Inc., Lincolnwood, IL

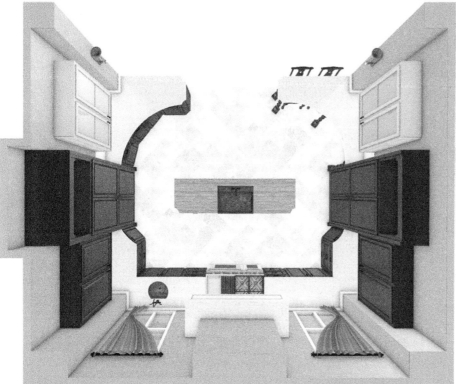

FIGURE 3.51 Kitchen with warm analogous color scheme

Design by Kristin Ann Okeley, CKD, codesigner Lisa Stites, Kitchens by Design, Indianapolis, IN
Brian Bookwalter Photography

FIGURE 3.52 Bathroom with warm analogous color scheme
Design by Tess E. Giuliani, CKD, Tess Giuliani Designs, Inc., Ridgewood, NJ Peter Rymwid Photography

treatment, wood and stone tones, along with orange in the copper and pottery as the predominant colors. In Figure 3.52, the colors of the warm reds, oranges, yellows, to yellow green in the wall tile mosaic, accented by the golden brass vanity bowl and accessories, create a warm analogous color scheme. The cool analogous colors of aqua (blue green), green, and yellow green in the wall tile and window shade fabric are repeated in the table setting as shown in the kitchen in Figure 3.53. Similarly, in Figure 3.54, versions of blue and blue green in the tub mosaic and shower curtain create a cool calming atmosphere in this bathroom.

Triad Color Scheme

Color schemes in which three colors are used that are equidistant from one another on the color wheel is a triad scheme. For example, the three primaries (yellow, blue, and red) may be used in their intense versions to create a happy, light, or cheerful theme, as seen in the kitchen in Figure 3.55. The primary colors of red, yellow, and blue in pure and related hues on both the cabinetry and glassware display create a vibrant, whimsical kitchen. The mosaic tile pattern in the shower and wall in Figure 3.56 also illustrate a less intense, calmer triadic color scheme in a bathroom.

Complementary Color Scheme

A scheme that features colors directly opposite one another on the color wheel is called complementary. One color is usually warm, and the other is usually cool. To use a complementary

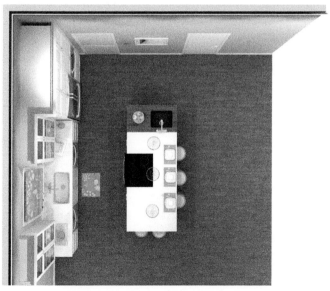

FIGURE 3.53 Kitchen with cool analogous color scheme

*Design by Cheryl Kees Clendenon, codesigner Stacy Snowden, In Detail Interiors, Pensacola, FL
Greg Riegler Photography*

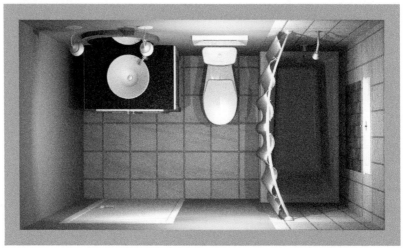

FIGURE 3.54 Bathroom with cool analogous color scheme

Design by Cheryl Kees Clendenon, In Detail Interiors, Pensacola, FL
Photo by Greg Riegler

FIGURE 3.55 Kitchen with triad color scheme
Design by Pietro Giorgi, Sr., CMKBD and Ellen Cheever, CMKBD, ASID, Wilmington, DE
Photo by McClain Imagery

scheme successfully, to the designer usually tries to maintain the natural value of the colors (or close to it), although that is not always necessary. The kitchen in Figure 3.57 successfully uses the intense fuchsia red with the bright green cabinetry as the dominant colors to create the contrast in an active family kitchen. In the bathroom shown in Figure 3.58, the complementary colors of purple and yellow/gold are used.

Neutral (Achromatic) Color Scheme

A neutral or achromatic scheme, by strict definition, is considered to possess no definable hue. In this color scheme, primarily black, white, and gray are used. In today's design, however, this definition has been expanded to include beige, taupe, and brown as neutrals as well. An accent of a single brilliant color with one or more of the neutrals is often used to create an interesting vibrant combination and add some contrast. Generally doing this will not overwhelm even a small kitchen or bathroom. However, recently it has become popular to create both kitchens and bathrooms that adhere to the strict definition of neutrals, white and black, often with some gray (see Figures 3.59 and 3.60). The kitchen in Figure 3.61 uses a variety of beige/taupe/brown neutral tones, from dark to light, in the variety of brown tones of the woods, the black of the countertop, and silver gray of the appliances and faucets. In

FIGURE 3.56 Bathroom with triad color scheme

Design by Elina Katsioula-Beall, CKD, codesigner Karen Frid-Madden, Dewitt Designer Kitchens, Pasadena, CA
Photo by Suki Medencevic

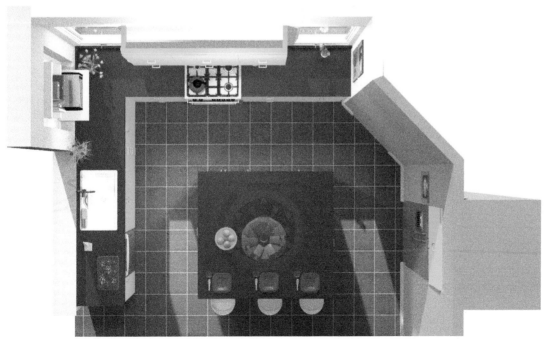

FIGURE 3.57 Kitchen with a complementary color scheme
Design by Elina Katsioula-Beall, CKD, Dewitt Designer Kitchens, Pasadena, CA
Photo by Suki Medencevic

FIGURE 3.58 Bathroom with complementary color scheme
Design by Tess Giuliani, CKD, Tess Giuliani Designs, Inc., Ridgewood, NJ

the bathroom shown in Figure 3.62, the dark brown and medium brown tones of the cabinetry is contrasted with the lighter off-white tone of the countertop, tied together with the inclusion of all these tones in the small mosaic wall tile.

Color and Its Emotional Impact

Colors have an emotional impact on the viewer and user of a space and vary from person to person. Rebecca Ewing, a color specialist in Atlanta, Georgia, (www.handsonhues.com), offers seminars on color for designers. The following is a review of how she perceives specific colors typically affect people.

Yellow

According to Rebecca Ewing, a color specialist in Atlanta, GA "Yellow can increase irritability, especially if bright or in a large quantity. Exercise care if the client is short-tempered. Yellow also stimulates the appetite and enhances memory retention (think of a yellow legal pad, yellow highlighter, or yellow Post-it Note ™)."

Yellow will always remain an important part of the kitchen palette because it is sunny, bright, and a happy color that works well with the natural color of food products. Whether a buttery golden tone reflecting the creamy sense of meringues or a punchy, vibrant look reminiscent of a bouquet of daffodils, yellow can wash across the cabinets or be used as an accent. Yellow has become more intriguing recently as it entered the world of metallic golden tones.

Green

"The eyes see green as a neutral, "says Ewing." And the body perceives it as a neutral. It's a suburban color indicating moderation, temperate behavior. In that it is the color of the earth, it provides true balance."

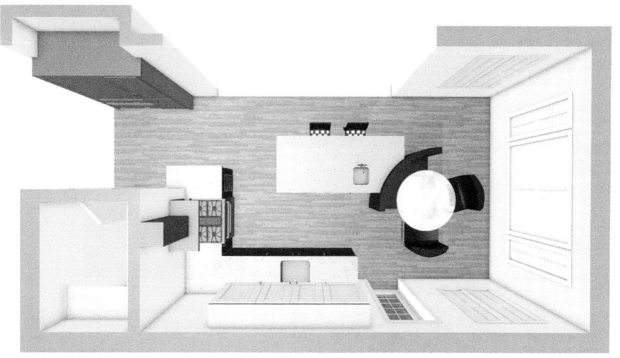

FIGURE 3.59 Kitchen with a neutral color scheme, white and black

Design by Beverley Leigh Binns, Binns Kitchen + Bath Design, Pickering, ON
Photo by Tim McClean

FIGURE 3.60 Bathroom with a neutral color scheme, white, black, gray

Design by Leslie Lamarre, CKD, codesigner Erika Shjeflo, TRG Architects, Burlingame, CA
Photo by Bernard Andre Photography

Green can be used as a dark, yellow or blue green that has been inspired by nature and its serenity as well as a mauve silver green that works well with neutrals and complementary colors. In the past, green was sometimes avoided, seen as a uniform or work clothing color and not very flattering to most skin tones. Today, it's a fresh, embraceable hue. It is often used as a neutral backdrop behind a stronger accent color.

Blue

"Blue reminds us of water. It slows the body system down; we feel we have all the time in the world. It is the color of logic, leading one to think conceptually. And good news, dieters: it depresses the appetite," affirms Ewing.

Blue—awash with white—continues to be a strong color preference and is popular in both kitchens and bathrooms and among both women and men. Navy or dark, rich blues are often specified for long-term living environments. Blue is an excellent complementary color to the variety of orange hues seen in ginger, cinnamon, or honey tones in other surfaces. Lighter, washed denim blue is another variation on the use of this color.

Violet

According to Rebecca Ewing: "Violet is a regal color oftentimes associated with the spiritual, with wealth, and with stature," and it is a perennial favorite of baby boomers.

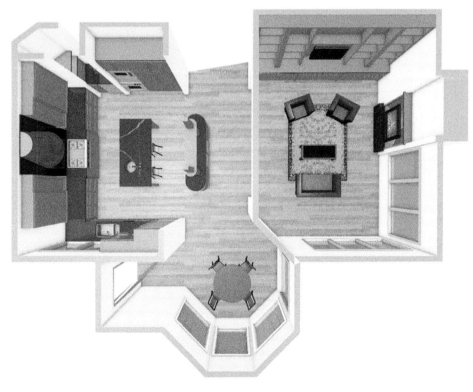

FIGURE 3.61 Kitchen with a neutral color scheme, beiges and browns

Design by Siri Evju, CKD, CBD, Siri Designs, Portland, OR
Photo by Manier Creative

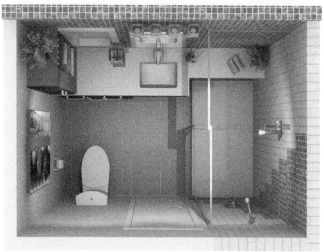

FIGURE 3.62 Bathroom with a neutral color scheme, beiges and browns

Design by Terence Tung, codesigner Joseph Irons, CGR, GMB, CAPS, CGP, Kitchen Craft Cabinetry, Newcastle, WA Photo by Tom Redner

Home fashion leaders, the European press, and some women clothiers continually predict that violet will be an emerging color in the future—but for most consumers, it's just too hard to live with permanently. It may be just right for an infrequently used yet dramatic guest powder room, or as an accent with accessories.

Reds and Pinks

"Red is the longest color wave, thus is seen before all others. Red lets us feel that we can focus on the impulse, indulge ourselves, have the courage or knowledge to be truly individualistic, and live for the present moment." People eat more and will pay more in a red environment.

Red is used frequently in fast-food restaurants to encouraging diners to eat more quickly so they can serve more customers and make more money. Interestingly enough, pink—a version of red—has a much different impact from its strong red foundation color. "A natural stress reducer, [pink] stimulates our interest in sweet, sugary things," says Ewing.

Red is used extensively in the fashion world to anchor black. It is an excellent accent color and is seen in dark, vibrant, merlot-type finishes on woods and in some solid surfacing and quartz countertop materials.

Oranges and Browns

"Orange has never had much 'snob appeal,' yet is much loved. Orange is playful, fun, and pleasurable."

Global color trends are leading designers to see a new use of intense orange tones in heavily structured geometric patterns emerging from the African and South American communities. This interest in orange is moving the color into a deeper, richer tone.

Browns—in many cases simply a tone of orange or a dark yellow—are safe colors, often specified by the ultraconservative. Ewing finds that those who love brown find it safe and nurturing, and those who hate it find it dull and boring. However, they are given a new life as they become textural mixed with metallics. The dark, earthy brown colors of oak and cherry are used in the furniture world. The wide variety of brown tones is returning to popularity in kitchen and bathroom settings.

Other Color Considerations

As a designer, there are other emotional and perceptual considerations to think about when selecting colors for clients. Color selection is very personal, and not everyone reacts in the same way to any given color. It is important that as the designer, you understand your client's color preferences early in the project. Preferences for colors are influenced by several factors: environment (both natural and man-made), cultural background, age, and life experiences. In addition, understanding some of the perceptual considerations of color is important to assist you the designer in achieving the design goals for a project and are listed below:

- Through the advancing properties of the color, use warm colors and shades to make a room seem smaller and warmer or to make an object in the room seem bigger.
- Through the receding properties of the color, use cool colors to make the room seem bigger and more restful or to make an object appear smaller.
- Use light colors to decrease the weight of an object or objects and thus to increase the overall perception of space.
- Use dark colors to increase the weight of an object and to decrease the perception of space in the total area.
- Use the same color or closely related colors throughout an area to camouflage structural problems or irregularities.
- Use heavily textured surfaces to absorb light and dull the intensity of a color if you wish to decrease apparent size and add warmth to the item.
- Use smooth, shiny surfaces to reflect light and to intensify the color of an object, which will also increase its apparent size.

If you wish to create a spatial illusion by using color, try these color techniques.

- To expand space via color:
  - Use cool colors.
  - Use light colors.
  - Use dull colors.
  - Keep contrasts to a minimum.
- To shrink space with color:
  - Use warm colors.
  - Use dark colors.
  - Use bright colors.
  - Introduce several contrasts.
- To lower a ceiling with color:
  - Use warm colors.
  - Use dark tones.
  - Use strong saturation.
- To heighten a ceiling with color:
  - Use cool colors.
  - Use light tints.
- To shorten a room with color, on the narrow wall of the room:
  - Use warm colors.
  - Use dark colors.
  - Use a strong saturation.
- To lengthen a room with color:
  - Use cool colors.
  - Use light colors.
  - Use dull colors.
  - Limit contrasts.

A Final Comment on the Importance of Color

For years, design wisdom has been to use simple, quiet colors on major surfaces, saving intense, vibrant tones, tints, and shades as accents. The use of color can be a counterpoint to this safe use of neutrals and gentler colors.

Global economic power shifts plus worldwide communications have led to a shift in design leadership (including color trends) from the Western European community, which has always looked toward soft neutral color palettes in hard goods and home furnishings. Although we are still strongly influenced by Western European styling today there are also strong influences from Africa, Asia, the Middle East, and from the Mediterranean and Central and South American countries, resulting in greater variety and more vibrant colors in interiors.

What is the importance of color to clients? A recent Yankelovich (a leading consumer market research and analytics company) survey indicated 39 percent of consumers are likely to change brands of a product if they can't get the color they want. That's proof of the power of color.

LIGHT

Light is the element of design that influences and affects the other design elements, especially color, often dramatically. Without light, there is no color. It is a critical tool for any design scheme, yet it often it is not given the consideration it deserves and many times it is an afterthought in the planning process.

There are two major sources of light, natural and artificial, each with its own identifiable characteristics. Natural light can be bright or overcast. It varies with the time of day, size and location of windows, season of the year, climate and weather, geographic location, and the amount of shade, roof overhangs, and orientation of the room (north, south, east, or west). Artificial light sources vary with color temperature, type of lamp (i.e., incandescent, fluorescent, light-emitting diode [LED]), and intensity of the light output. Light can make a space appear large or small, expansive or intimate. Light colors tend to reflect light; dark colors absorb light. Thus, more lighting typically is required in a space with predominantly dark surfaces than with lighter ones. Light can change the apparent size, shape, or form of an object or room and influence the way colors, textures, and surfaces look and are interpreted. Simply by changing the color temperature of the lamps (bulbs) in fixtures, the colors in the space often appear different.

Because of the nature of and variety of activities performed in both kitchens and bathrooms, combinations of natural light sources along with artificial sources need to be considered. There are three categories of artificial lighting: general or ambient lighting, task lighting, and decorative/accent lighting to consider in these spaces. Some considerations for lighting decisions are mentioned next.

Selected considerations for lighting kitchens and bathrooms
- Function of and activities to be accomplished in space
- Size of space, ceiling height as well as floor area dimensions
- Users of space—including gender, ages (as one ages, more light is needed), any special needs
- Color and materials selections
- Natural light sources:
  - Windows, skylights: number, sizes, location, compass orientation
  - Geographic location, seasons, climate
  - Eaves, overhangs, shade trees, as applicable
- Artificial light sources:
  - Ambient/general lighting needs
  - Task lighting needs—list specific tasks
  - Decorative/accent lighting needs
- Energy and code requirements:
  - Fixture and lamp requirements
  - Color temperature and light output of lamps and luminaires

The NKBA *Kitchen and Bath Lighting* book and applicable chapters in *Kitchen Planning*, *Bath Planning*, and *Kitchen and Bath Residential Construction and Systems* discuss the specifics of light and lighting in kitchens and bathrooms in detail.

SUMMARY

This chapter presents and discusses the elements of design—line, shape, pattern, space, form, texture, color, and light, which are the tools used by designers to create aesthetically pleasing designs. Examples of the application of each of these elements to the design of kitchens and bathrooms are also presented.

REVIEW QUESTIONS

1. Name and define each of the eight elements of design. (See chapter introduction, page 27)
2. Describe the effect on a kitchen and bathroom space of the use of different kinds of line. (See "Line" pages 29–39)
3. Name and describe the different types of pattern. (See "Identifying Pattern Preferences" pages 52–62.)
4. Describe some of the effects of color in kitchens and bathrooms. (See "Color" pages 68–92)
5. Describe some of the effects of light that need to be considered in kitchens and bathrooms. (See "Light" pages 92–93)

Principles of Design

The individual tools of design (design elements discussed in Chapter 3) need to be organized and arranged in a logical and aesthetically pleasing manner to achieve the desired effect for the client. The principles of design provide the designer with a guidebook as to how to combine these elements to achieve this. They are the abstract concepts, the theory that determines the success (or failure) of a design. As both kitchens and bathrooms have gained importance and integration in the total home design scheme, understanding and the appropriate application of the elements and principles of design is critical to creating spaces clients desire and love, spaces that are aesthetically pleasing as well as functional. Typically, when a space or room does not seem to work or look quite right, often one or more of the design elements or principles has not been utilized correctly.

The six principles of design are:

1. Balance
2. Rhythm
3. Scale
4. Proportion
5. Emphasis/focal point
6. Harmony/unity

Each of these design principles is discussed with examples of kitchen and bathroom applications.

Learning Objective 1: Name and define each of the principles of design.

Learning Objective 2: Identify the application of symmetrical, asymmetrical, and radial balance.

Learning Objective 3: Identify the application of different types of rhythm.

Learning Objective 4: Identify proper and improper use of scale.

Learning Objective 5: Identify proper and improper examples of proportion.

Learning Objective 6: Identify and create a focal point or area of emphasis.

BALANCE

Balance is about presenting a vista to the viewer that offers different areas of equal interest to the eye. This means bringing equilibrium or stability to the space. Balance is employed to the left and right of a center point and at the top and bottom of an elevation or wall area. Studies have found that people react most favorably to the visually heavier-weighted objects at the lower section of the room. This is one reason why often darker colors or more patterned materials seen at the floor line are more satisfactory than heavy, vibrantly colored ceiling surfaces. Generally, one type dominates and is the primary balance used in a space, but that does not preclude the use of the other types subordinately. Unequal amounts tend to work best. There are three types of balance to consider and employ when planning a kitchen or bathroom:

1. Symmetrical or formal balance
2. Asymmetrical or informal balance
3. Radial balance

Symmetrical Balance

Symmetrical balance occurs when two (or a majority of) objects or elements of the room are exactly the same on either side of an imaginary centerline, often identified as a mirror image of one another. It is also thought to be more formal due to this sameness on each side, and usually is associated with more sophisticated, traditional, formal rooms and room settings. Balance is obtained by identical or very similar objects exerting equal thrust because of their placement and similar distance from the center of balance. Too much symmetrical balance can be uninteresting and is not usual in most kitchens and bathrooms. Some symmetrical balance, such as on one or two wall elevations, gives the appearance of stability to the space. For example, in a kitchen, equal size and number of cabinet doors on each side of the sink (or a range hood) create a symmetrically balanced elevation and are commonly seen. Figure 4.1 is an example of this type of symmetrical balance in the arrangement of cabinets on either side of the window above the sink. In bathroom planning, installing tall and equal shelves to flank each side of a tub and window area creates symmetrical balance along the wall, as illustrated in Figure 4.2. In each of these spaces, the symmetrical balance gives a sense of stability and sophistication.

Asymmetrical Balance

When unequal elements attract equal attention because of their placement, the resulting equilibrium is called asymmetrical or informal balance. Because of this difference, this type of balance is usually more interesting than symmetrical balance, especially if it is done well, and typically it is associated with more casual, informal rooms. In a kitchen (see Figure 4.3), a wall cabinet with glass doors and the large refrigerator/freezer are asymmetrically balanced by the open shelves and pass-through opening on the adjoining wall on the other side of the range and hood. In a bathroom setting (see Figure 4.4), the vanity arrangement illustrates asymmetrical balance with the bowl and mirror on one side balanced by the higher drawer unit and open view through the closet into the bedroom on the other.

Radial Balance

A third type of balance is created when equal (or nearly equal) objects attract equal attention as they radiate out from a central axis, in either a circle or a section of one. Radial balance is less frequently found in kitchen and bathroom design. In a kitchen, it is often used in some type of seating (usually with a curve) arrangement or island design. In the bathroom, an example of radial balance is a circular fixture in the center of the room. If you have an opportunity to employ radial balance, select and place one element of the room in the center—for example, an oversize island with seating in a kitchen or other entertainment area (see Figure 4.5) or a curved wall with the vanity bowl and flat space radiating out from it that draws the eye to the bowl (see Figure 4.6)—and then place all the other elements of the room radiating out from that central point.

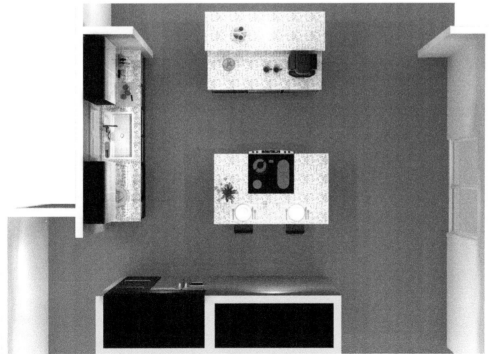

FIGURE 4.1 Kitchen designed with symmetrical balance

Design by Cheryl Hamilton-Gray, CKD, Hamilton-Gray Design Inc., Carlsbad, CA
Photo by Preview First

FIGURE 4.2 Bathroom designed with symmetrical balance

Design by Brigitte Fabi, CMKBD, Drury Design Kitchen & Bath Studio, Glen Ellyn, IL
Photo by Eric Hausman

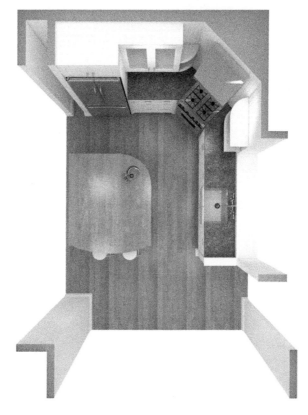

FIGURE 4.3 Kitchen designed with asymmetrical balance

Design by Jessica Williamson, Kitchen Views Custom, Newton, MA
Photo by Judson Abts Photography

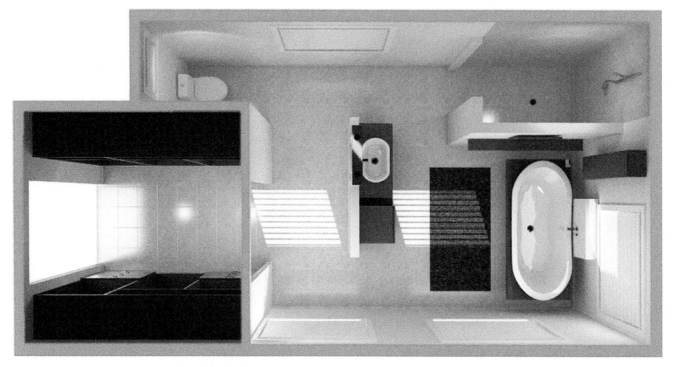

FIGURE 4.4 Bathroom designed with asymmetrical balance

Design by Elizabeth A. Rosensteel, codesigner Meredith Comfort, Elizabeth A. Rosensteel Design/Studio, LLC, Phoenix, AZ Photo by Robert Reck

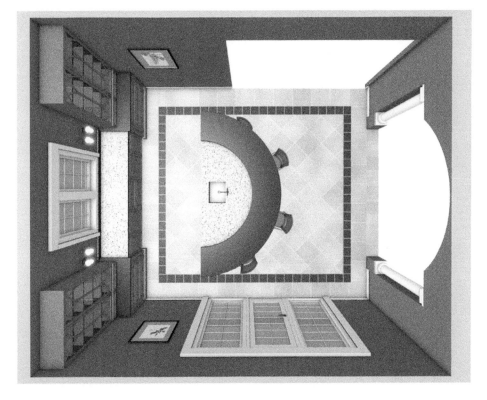

FIGURE 4.5 Entertainment area
designed with radial balance
*Design by Sandra L. Steiner-Houck,
CKD Steiner & Houck, Inc., Columbia,
PA*
Photo by Peter Leach Photography

FIGURE 4.6 Bathroom designed with radial balance

Design by Lori W. Carroll, NCIDQ/ASID, codesigners Guillermo Bazua and Mary Roles, Lori Carrol & Associates, Tucson, AZ
Photo by William Lesch

FIGURE 4.7 Kitchen with rhythm created by repetitious design

Design by Joseph A. Giorgi, Jr., CKD, codesigners Erin Paige Pitts and Dru Hinterleiter, Giorgi Kitchens & Designs, Wilmington, DE Photo by Peter Leach

RHYTHM

How often do you look at a room and intuitively feel it flows or "works" or note that although individual elements may be attractive, the overall room doesn't seem to fit together? If a room does work, it is most likely because its individual elements have been arranged in a rhythmic way. If not, the room probably is merely a collection of well-designed but dissimilar elements having no continuity in the way they flow or relate to one another.

The continuity or rhythm within a design is the glue that holds the dissimilar elements together, allowing the eye to move smoothly around the space. It is what helps to create the unified, total design. Continuity or rhythm is a matter of forms and lines that divide the space into understandable, logical, and usually predictable intervals. Rhythm is obtained in three major ways:

1. Repetition
2. Alternation
3. Progression or gradation

Repetition

Repetition is created when one or more design elements (lines, shapes, forms, colors, textures, or patterns) are repeated. The viewer's eye will follow the repeated element around the space.

For example, the repetition of the pendant light fixtures, drawer and cabinet pulls as well as the rectangular shape of the cabinetry (see Figure 4.7) moves the viewer's eye around the room. In a bathroom (see Figure 4.8), drawer hardware and shower fixtures provide rhythm through repetition of the square shape.

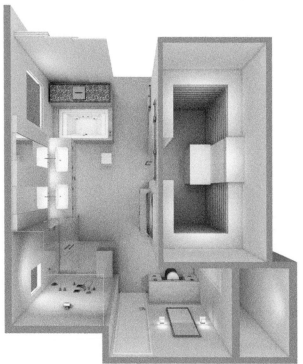

FIGURE 4.8 Bathroom with rhythm created by repetitious design

Design by Ada Pagano, A. Pagano Design, Inc., St. Petersburg, FL Photo by Everett & Soule

FIGURE 4.9 Kitchen with rhythm created by alternation
Design by Jamieson D. Simpson, CKD, Harrell Remodeling, Inc., Mountain View, CA

Alternation

The selected repeating of usually two motifs or objects pulls and holds the design together by providing a logical step, moving the eye from one element to the next. The principle of alternation is often used in decorative tile backsplash or floor designs in kitchens and bathrooms. For example, in kitchen design, a parquet hardwood floor or similarly patterned tile floor may provide an alternating rhythm through the space, possibly in a checkerboard fashion (see Figure 4.9). Or a surfacing material or objects, such as wall sconces and mirrors (see Figure 4.10), are used throughout a space with a decorative alternate pattern that creates a rhythmic design. It may be a stripe, a geometric element, or simply a change in color or pattern. A change in color from the edge, to deck, to backsplash in solid surface countertop finishes is another example.

Progression/Gradation

With progression or gradation, a motif, design, or shape progresses through a series of usually gradual intermediate steps that carry the eye from one end of the scale to the other, generally from small to large or vice versa (see Figure 4.11). The shape, size, or even motif itself changes in small increments. (See Figure 4.12, where cabinet drawers get progressively smaller from the bottom up, and Figure 4.13, with the candles and guest towel holder arrangements.) Gradations (or a progressive change) of colors from dominant shades to more subdued hints can also be effective and are another example of a type of progression.

Another example of progressive rhythm are changes in square or rectangular floor elements from larger to smaller size at the deck or backsplash.

FIGURE 4.10 Bathroom with rhythm created by alternation

Design by Paul Knutson, Knutson Residential Design, LLC, Saint Paul, MN Photo by Troy Thies

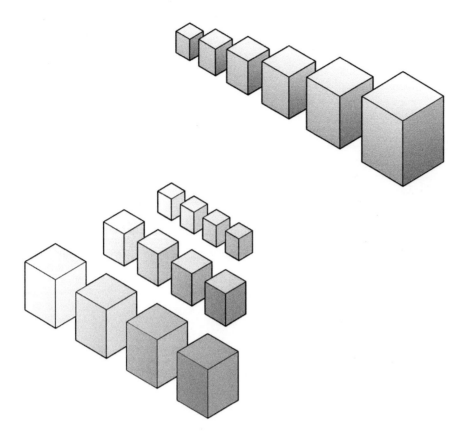

FIGURE 4.11 Diagram of progressive rhythm

SCALE AND PROPORTION

The two design principles of scale and proportion are discussed together because they are closely related and often are confused by designers and clients alike. They both involve design relationships. Scale deals with size relationships of objects within and to an entire space. Proportion deals with space division relationships, generally within a specific object or area, such as a wall elevation.

Scale

Scale refers to the overall size (largeness or smallness) of a room and the relationship of the objects in it to one another and the space as a whole. It is a relative issue, dependent on known sizes of both the space and objects to be used within it. Reference to human scale is important in interior design, and especially for kitchens and bathrooms. The human scale should be used as a guide to select objects that fit the needs and functions of users as well as the space. Although certain standards have become the norm for both kitchens and bathrooms, such as counter height and depth, often kitchen and bath designers adjust the size (and consequently scale) to best accommodate users. Scale also depends on the actual size of the space. Generally it is easier to achieve appropriate and pleasing scale in large spaces (i.e., selecting large appliances in a kitchen, a large soaking tub or spa in a bathroom) and often more challenging in small spaces (i.e., fitting in everything that is desired, necessary, and fits the user), not unusual situations in kitchens and bathrooms. There is a wide range of different sizes available for appliances, cabinetry, and fixtures from which to select for this reason. The designer's goal is to have appropriately scaled items for each room, have them fit the users and the space, function, have them be aesthetically pleasing, and ensure they satisfy the client's needs. This can be particularly challenging when the client wants to include more than can be accommodated or items that are too large for the existing or planned space.

FIGURE 4.12 Kitchen with rhythm created by progression/gradation

Design by Lilley Yee, CMKBD, CID, ASID, Lilley Yee Interiors, San Mateo, CA
Photography Copyright Dean J. Birinyi, ASMP

FIGURE 4.13 Bathroom with rhythm created by progression/gradation

Design by Sandra L. Steiner-Houck, CKD, Steiner & Houck, Inc., Columbia, PA
Peter Leach Photography

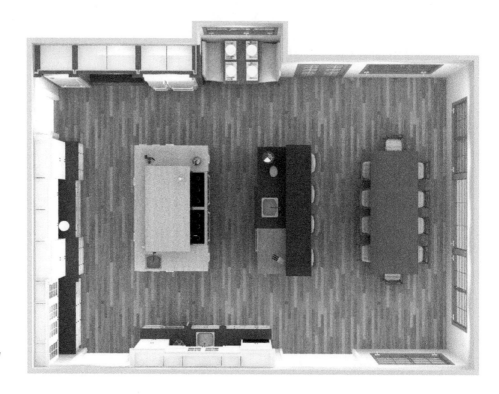

FIGURE 4.14 Appropriate scale in a kitchen

Design by Peter Ross Salerno, CMKBD, Peter Salerno Inc., Wyckoff, NJ
Photo by Peter Rymwid Architectural Photography

An example of appropriate scaled items for a large kitchen is shown in Figure 4.14; the large space can easily accommodate the large island and hood above it in addition to the large appliances and ample storage. In the bathroom in Figure 4.15, appropriately scaled items are selected that suit the small space.

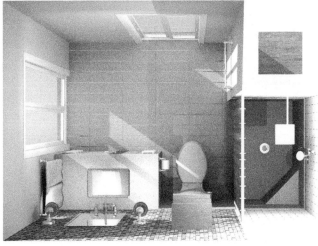

FIGURE 4.15 Appropriate scale in a bathroom

Design by Leslie Lamarre, CKD, codesigner Erika Shjeflo, TRG Architects, Burlingame, CA
Photo by Bernard Andre Photography

FIGURE 4.16 Kitchen with good proportions

Design by Thomas David Trzcinski, CMKBD, Kitchen & Bath Concepts of Pittsburgh, LLC, Pittsburgh, PA
Photo by Craig Thompson Photography

Proportion

Proportion refers to the space division relationships within an object or specific space, such as an elevation view. An object can be scaled appropriately for a room but have poor proportions. Likewise, an object can have good proportions but be out of scale for the particular room.

The Western ideal of good proportion has been the Greek Golden Mean, the two-to-three relationship between sides of an object or space divisions within it. It has become the goal (or approaching it) when designing objects and rooms. When faced with a square room, designers generally seek to lengthen one side and make the room appear to be more rectangular. Likewise, when faced with a long narrow room, designers attempt to shorten the length and expand the width to achieve the appearance of a desirable, more rectangular shape. With appliances and cabinetry, considering the proportions for each wall elevation is important to give a sense of stability and belonging along the wall as well as in the space, larger divisions on the bottom, smaller ones up above. In the kitchen in Figure 4.16, the lower and upper cabinets have the larger division at the bottom, approximating this two-thirds to one-third relationship. The bathroom in Figure 4.17 shows the same relationship in the frosted glass floor to ceiling cabinets.

EMPHASIS: THE FOCAL POINT

The next principle of design involves the overall center of interest in the room. The focal point in the design is carefully crafted so the viewer's eye is drawn to it easily, usually immediately upon entering the space. To create a focal point within a space, designers strive to include three levels of attention-grabbing design: dominant, subdominant, and subordinate. A dominant focal point captures the sense of the space, and the viewer should notice that first when entering, often by its size or contrast to the rest of the space. A second layer of subdominant elements is not as important as the key element, but it supports and accents that key element. Subordinate elements add definition to the total design without overwhelming or competing with the main focal point.

Typically two types of emphasis (focal point) are used in kitchens and bathrooms: area emphasis and theme emphasis.

Area Emphasis

Emphasizing or drawing attention to one area is particularly appropriate in creating a focal point in both kitchens and bathrooms. The key is to decide what that area in the room will be. The designer (or client) may wish to highlight the range/hood or view window area in a kitchen or the vanity or spa tub area in a bathroom. In many designs today, a kitchen sink cabinet literally protrudes beyond the adjacent cabinetry, with a unique treatment framing a window above. This creates a center of interest as one enters the space. The same type of unique treatment is used as a backsplash in range and hood areas, often introducing a contrasting color (see Figure 4.18). The vanity or closet area in a bathroom, a luxurious spa tub arrangement framed by windows, or unique or contrasting wall surface treatments are ideal spots to create area emphasis in this space. In Figure 4.19, the shoe storage shelf with its dramatic color contrast is an example in the bathroom/dressing area.

Theme Emphasis

The designer also can create emphasis by allowing the surface selections or the specific style of the space to dominate the room. This is often seen in detailed rooms where the dominant pattern of a material, style, a specific shape, or woodworking details create a cohesive environment that often follow a particular style, from either a historical period or a specific cultural style. Some of these themes are discussed in detail in Chapters 5 and 6.

FIGURE 4.17 Bathroom with good proportions

Design by Yuko Matsumoto, CKD, CBD, Altera Design & Remodeling Inc., Walnut Creek, CA
Photo by Douglas Johnson Photography

FIGURE 4.18 Area emphasis in a kitchen, the back splash/cooktop area

Design by Jonas Carnemark, CKD, Carnemark, Bethesda, MD
Photo by Anice Hoachlander

FIGURE 4.19 Area emphasis in a bathroom, the shoe display/storage

Design by Shea Pumarejo, Younique Designs, Helotes, TX

Photo by Casey Dunn

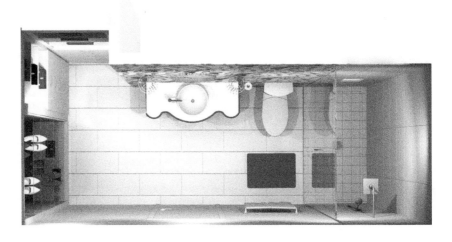

Not all themes are based on a particular time period or culture. Two of these are rustic and naturalistic. The kitchen seen in Figure 4.20 illustrates a rustic theme: The rustic wood cabinetry of a country farmhouse from an earlier time and the curved shape of the hood dominate the space, supported by repeating the similar curve of the peninsula, display niche, and pendant luminaires. Another theme, naturalistic, is carried throughout the bathroom seen in Figure 4.21 with a pebble mosaic floor, rough wood branch-framed mirror, and animal form accessories, giving a feeling of being part of the out-of-doors.

FIGURE 4.20 Theme emphasis—kitchen

Design by James Howard, CKD, CBD, codesigners Steve Levin and Sonja Willman, Glen Alspaugh Company, St. Louis, MO
Photo by Alise O'Brien Photography

FIGURE 4.21 Theme emphasis—bathroom

Design by Tess Giuliani, CKD, Tess Giuliani Designs, Inc., Ridgewood, NJ
Photo Peter Rymwid Architectural Photography

FIGURE 4.22 Kitchen with harmony/unity

Design by Anastasia Rentzos, CKD, CBD, Andros Kitchen & Bath Designs, Mississauga, ON
Photo by Averill Lehan/PAI

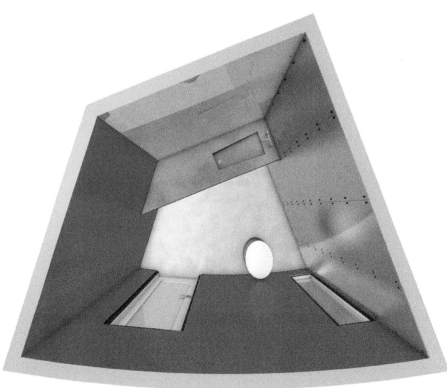

FIGURE 4.23 Bathroom with harmony/unity

Design by Lori Carroll, codesigner Mary Roles, Lori Carroll & Associates, Tucson, AZ
Photo by William Lesch Photography

HARMONY/UNITY

Harmony (or unity) is the ultimate goal of any design: the creation of a cohesive space that both functions well and is aesthetically pleasing. This is achieved by incorporating the elements of design (discussed in Chapter 3) and following the principles of design discussed in this chapter. A successful design typically consists of the appropriate application and use of the elements and principles of design as seen in each of these spaces (see Figures 4.22 and 4.23). When the design of a space does not seem to work or look quite right, taking a step back and analyzing it usually uncovers an inappropriate application or use of one or more of the elements and/or principles of design.

SUMMARY

It is important to note that good design is not an accident. No matter how small or challenging the kitchen or bathroom, the design is a major part of the planning process. The space needs to be pleasing to the eye as well as functionally well planned. Ideally, it should be created so it is lasting and stands the test of time.

A good way to understand this sense of timeless design is to consider the difference between style and fashion. Being in fashion means being willing to listen to others dictate what is "in" or beautiful. Style is much more lasting. It is about being free to design because of the solution's appropriateness for the environment and the client. Whereas fashion encloses or defines, style invites. Whereas fashion demands acceptance, style is individualized. Fashion so often seems just a moment too new or, at worst, just a moment too old. Style moves forward with ease and timeless grace.

Fashion is not to be ignored. It is a designer's tool and occasionally an influence, but it should not be considered a dictate. Employing the elements and principles of design will assist you, the designer, in building a stylish environment that is well suited to the client, that will stand the test of time and be functional, and that still will be considered beautiful years after the project is completed.

Understanding the principles of design as well as the elements discussed in Chapter 3 and being able to apply them to design situations is critical for kitchen and bathroom designers. They are as important to the overall design as meeting the functional requirements for the space.

REVIEW QUESTIONS

1. Name and define each of the principles of design. (See page 95)
2. Give an example of the application of symmetrical, asymmetrical, and radial balance in kitchens and bathrooms. (See "Balance" page 96)
3. Identify the application of different types of rhythm in kitchens and bathrooms. (See "Rhythm" pages 103–105)
4. Give an example of good use of scale in kitchens and bathrooms. (See "Scale" pages 107– 111)
5. Identify an example of good use of proportion in kitchens and bathrooms. (See "Proportion" page 113)
6. What does one consider to create a focal point in a kitchen and bathrooms? (See "Emphasis: The Focal Point" pages 113–117)

Historic Style Influences to the Late Nineteenth Century

This chapter is an overview of selected historic period style themes and influences that are used in residential interiors, beginning with the ancient styles of Europe, through the nineteenth century. The focus is on some of the most commonly used European and American historic and vernacular (regional) architectural and interior design influences, with examples of how selected styles can be incorporated into the design of kitchens and bathrooms. Chapter 6 focuses on the historic styles and themes from the late nineteenth century to the present time and how they, too, can be applied to kitchen and bathroom design. Selected global, cultural, and other worldwide design style themes and design applications are discussed in Chapter 7. Those desiring further information and more specific details related to these and other historic and worldwide design styles not covered in these chapters are encouraged to refer to bibliographical references, both print and Internet Web sites, for this chapter and Chapters 6 and 7 in the list of resources at the end of the book.

Learning Objective 1: Identify and apply the steps for creating a historic theme for a kitchen or bathroom project.

Learning Objective 2: Identify significant European and American historic architectural and interior design styles from ancient times through the nineteenth century used in residential design.

Learning Objective 3: Apply characteristics of a selected historic style to the design of kitchens and bathrooms.

ESTABLISHING A HISTORIC THEME FOR A KITCHEN OR BATHROOM PROJECT

Once the designer has an understanding of the elements and principles of design, the next step in adapting generic design training to a specific kitchen and bathroom planning situations is to understand how to create rooms that follow a style or theme, such as a historical or specific cultural theme, or incorporate key elements of current modern interiors into their design. Not all clients want to follow a specific historical or cultural theme, but it has become more common since World War II for clients with homes from a specific historical architectural style—whether new construction, renovation, or a remodel—to follow that style throughout the interior, including in the design of the kitchen and bathroom.

Clients may show designers a picture that is reminiscent of a historical or historically influenced structure, such as a cottage in the English, French, or American Victorian countryside, a sleek apartment in New York City, an early twentieth-century bungalow, or a mid-twentieth-century ranch house as inspiration for their design. Designers do not need to be experts in each of these design styles, but ideally they should have a good working knowledge of the history behind the styles and a basic understanding of the significant attributes of such spaces, which they can transfer to rooms created in the twenty-first century. They also need to be familiar with the vocabulary of design, the variety of terms, and their definitions. (See Appendixes A and B and the list of resources for additional, more detailed information.)

Designers along with client input establish a historic theme for the kitchen or bathroom as a way to assist them in developing and organizing the project. Once a definite style or theme influence is identified, many possibilities are automatically eliminated, and a more manageable range of choices can be presented to the client. This limiting of design options is important and ultimately can save time during the planning process. If clients are unsure of the style (or its name) that they would like to use, showing them picture examples of general interiors, as well as kitchens and bathrooms in different historic styles, can assist them in narrowing choices. Often clients already have their own set of pictures of interior spaces, including kitchens and bathrooms that they like (often reflecting specific periods or several styles), which are helpful to the designer.

Designers and clients sometimes wonder how to know what is appropriate for a specific architectural style. This question can be difficult to answer because there are few guidelines specific for kitchens and bathrooms to follow until the late nineteenth and early twentieth centuries. (Refer to Chapter 1, "A Brief History of Kitchen and Bathroom Design.")

Most architectural style periods have characteristic and distinctive furniture and interior (as well as exterior) architectural styles. Therefore, designers usually adapt a furniture or architectural style (or some of the elements) to cabinetry, then use characteristic colors, materials, motifs, and/or accessories associated with the period to give a feeling of the style. Designers must also contend with the functional requirements of modern appliances, kitchen and bathroom fixtures and fittings, and current building code and space requirements. Fortunately, in recent years, cabinet, fixture, and appliance manufacturers have developed product lines that are reminiscent of or blend with a variety of different historic style periods, making it easier for designers and clients to create the desired theme, look and feel, yet with all the modern technology and conveniences available.

The most practical recommendation to create a room reminiscent of the past is to strive for the feeling of the requested style or styles rather than an actual reproduction of the design and products of the period. The latter can be difficult, if not impossible, to achieve, as well as impractical for today's lifestyles.

To accomplish the desired historical look, designers need to understand the various architectural and historical interior styles; become familiar with the furniture styles, colors, motifs, materials, and fashions associated with each era; and translate this information successfully into a functional modern kitchen or bathroom with the appropriate period motifs and ambiance.

As kitchen and bathroom planners surf the Internet or leaf through magazines and see highly stylized interiors, they should realize that throughout its history, Western architecture has been identified with the character of Western civilization as well as being a reflection of it. It is important for designers to understand the context of the style and what it represents.

When studying the history of architecture, particularly home design, the specific periods of design, styles of architecture, and furniture need to be identified. These eras are commonly called period styles. Period styles are named and organized differently, depending on the source being referenced or country with which it is associated. Some styles cross over several periods or are included in more than one style category, which can be confusing to designers and clients alike. Each source has its own set of definitions, interpretations, and organization of information, adding to the confusion. This brief overview reflects in summary form what is taught in many history of interior design and architecture and art history courses at the postsecondary level. (They don't always agree.) To assist with the vocabulary and definitions of common terms, refer to Appendix B. Dates are approximate and subject to interpretation, so they serve primarily as points of reference. Most styles, with a few exceptions, evolve slowly, reach a height in popularity, and then gradually begin to wane, being replaced by yet another style. Some go away completely; others do not, enjoying a consistent or renewed popularity.

It is also worth noting that a majority of the architectural, interior, and furniture design styles mentioned here were for centuries the purview of the wealthy, nobility, and clergy rather than for the masses (or what would be considered today the average person). It wasn't until the eighteenth century that architectural and design styles and the beginnings of what is now considered the middle class began to emerge, with the middle class eventually becoming the majority of the population (in the United States). Design styles for architecture, furniture, and materials for the masses typically were simpler versions of what the wealthy had. These design or period styles go by several names, including "country" and "provincial" or use a regional vernacular term or a religious or specific sect name. Some of the more popular country styles are highlighted in this chapter.

ANCIENT/CLASSICAL PERIOD

The design vocabulary and theory that has shaped Western architecture and design began with ancient Greece (about 1000 BC) and lasted through the classical Roman period, and is characterized by a set of organized compositional rules, including balance, rhythm, scale, and proportion and significant architectural design elements, in particular columns and their orders, Doric, Ionic, and Corinthian (see Figure 5.1). There are also specific motifs first associated with the ancient Greeks, including a variety of architectural moldings, such as the dentil, egg and dart, fret, and acanthus leaf, to mention a few. These motifs and moldings are commonly used with styles with a classical, traditional feel and recur frequently throughout history.

Later, the Romans expanded on the Greek columns and other motifs as well. With their increasing engineering skill, they developed more sophisticated structural elements, including the arch and the dome. They also developed the formula for concrete, which enabled them to create more varied and larger structural buildings and more elaborate interpretations of the motifs borrowed from the Greeks.

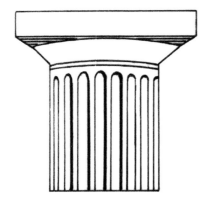 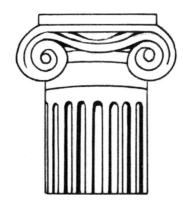 

DORIC   IONIC   CORINTHIAN

FIGURE 5.1 Greek orders of architecture

FIGURE 5.2 Roman-inspired bathroom (Kohler, Archer collection tub)
Courtesy of Kohler Company

Classical-Inspired Kitchens and Bathrooms

Although clients generally do not seek to re-create authentic ancient Greek or Roman kitchens or bathrooms, some would like the feeling and use the original, relatively simple ancient design elements that were popular among the wealthy during those times. For example, some large master bathrooms are designed to be reminiscent of an ancient Roman bath with the tub in the center of the room and symmetrical wall arrangements. (see Figure 5.2). Others incorporate modern fixtures, design materials, and fixtures but include ancient design motifs, such as the Greek key wall mosaic inspired by Greek pottery designs or the egg and dart and Ionic capital motifs seen in Figure 5.3. In kitchens, cabinetry that incorporates Classical design elements, typically including Greek- or Roman-style columns and moldings, scenic wall treatments, and usually symmetrical wall elevation arrangements give the feeling of either (or both) ancient Classical styles (see Figure 5.4).

Ancient Greek and Roman Classicism is a design language that has continually reinvented itself. It has provided successive generations the tools to explore and apply these

FIGURE 5.3 Use of the egg-and-dart and Ionic capital motifs
Courtesy of Wood-Mode Fine Custom Cabinetry

fundamentals of design, each with its own unique interpretations. Historically, Classicism (in some form) predominated in the architectural world from approximately 1000 BC into the sixth century as the influence of the Middle Ages was emerging. It served as a foundation for design guidelines during the Renaissance period (fifteenth into the seventeenth centuries), which was considered to be the "rebirth of or return to Classicism," with the rediscovery of the drawings and writings of the ancient Roman architect Vitruvius. It also served as a foundation for the Neoclassical (new Classic) late eighteenth- and early nineteenth-century European architecture and furniture designs that came about with the unearthing of the ruins of Pompeii and Herculaneum. Classicism influenced the Victorian Renaissance revival interpretation in the nineteenth century, using industrial technology and materials. In the late twentieth century Classicism influenced postmodern design. There are commonalities among all of these styles, with the underlying classical influences, and they are often used together. Each of these styles is covered chronologically in this chapter and in Chapter 6.

FIGURE 5.4 Roman-inspired kitchen
Courtesy of Colonial Craft Kitchens, Inc., Annville, PA
Photo by Robert Millman Photography

Greek- and Roman-inspired design elements:

Cabinetry/millwork. Rectilinear forms are based on the Greek "golden mean" relationship of 2:3. Straight lines and symmetry predominate. Classic columns, pilasters, and white, gray, or other light-colored cabinetry are used to simulate light marble or other stone.

Hardware/fixtures. Simple, straight lines and handles or round knobs are used. Iron or brushed metals in a variety of classical shapes prevail.

Countertops. Marble, granite, limestone, simulated marble, or stone finish (i.e., laminate, solid surfaces, engineered stone) are used for countertops.

Floors. Mosaic or large tiles, either ceramic or stone, or stone slabs are common for floors.

Walls. Textured or rough plaster, trompe l'oeil ("fool the eye") paintings or wallpapers are used on walls.

Ceilings and lighting. Ceilings are typically plaster with dark wood beams. Classically shaped (including those replicating a classical motif), symmetrical metal and glass lighting fixtures are common.

Colors. Neutrals (white, off-white, and gray predominate), from light to dark, are common, although it is not unusual to see more intense versions of a variety of primary and secondary colors (i.e., red, yellow, blue, green), derived primarily from nature and natural dye sources.

Representative motifs. These motifs are common: Greek key (or fret), egg and dart, bead and reel, dentil, wave, herringbone, honeysuckle, guilloche, acanthus leaf, anthemion, lotus bud, sphinx, obelisk, Greek and Roman column styles (as columns, supports, or pilasters), Roman arch, urns.

Fabrics. Cotton, linen, or wool, plain or slightly textured or patterns incorporating a classical design motif, are used.

Accents/accessories. Urns, classical statues, columns, scenes, and mosaics are popular.

Associated styles. Renaissance, Baroque, Georgian, Neoclassic styles of the eighteenth and nineteenth centuries, postmodern from the twentieth century, any style that incorporates Classical design motifs.

MIDDLE AGES/GOTHIC PERIOD

In structural terms, the creation of Gothic architecture during the later Middle Ages (beginning about the twelfth century into the fifteenth century) marked a major departure from what had gone on before as it had no roots in the design of Classicism. Gothic architecture was based on a sophisticated understanding of the way in which a minimum of structure could carry a maximum of load and add height. Visually, the pointed arch most frequently characterizes the Gothic period and its architecture. Because there was limited patronage of the arts, unstable governmental times, and the growth and establishment of the Christian religion in Europe during this period, architecture and design were directed primarily by religious leaders and institutions. Gothic architecture, believed to have first emerged in France and then spread to the rest of Europe, was also a physical expression of spiritual values. It is suffused with Christian symbolism and doctrine, a way to educate and direct the masses, who were largely illiterate during this time, through design.

The structures and motifs, primarily derived from churches and castles, of the Middle Ages and Gothic period influenced later architects and cabinetmakers. Some of these notably include Thomas Chippendale in the eighteenth century with his "Gothick" style and architects in the early nineteenth century with a Gothic version of Victorian design, which has had a limited influence on kitchen and bathroom design in the United States at the time. The influence of the Gothic style was felt in the last half of the twentieth century with a postmodern interpretation. The Gothic style, in its various forms, is still a widely used design style in contemporary homes, especially in England, and includes kitchens and bathrooms.

Gothic-Inspired Kitchens and Bathrooms

As with the ancient Greek and Roman style of kitchens and bathrooms, most clients do not seek to re-create an authentic medieval or Gothic kitchen or bathroom. Generally certain motifs are used to create the feeling of the design period. Elements used in kitchens and bathrooms are most often the Gothic arch and/or occasionally one of the foils, the trefoil or quatrefoil primarily in cabinet doors, both solid and with glass fronts (see Figures 5.5 and 5.6), moldings, and other millwork. In the bathroom, the Gothic arch is often seen in fixture designs and are especially popular in England.

Gothic-inspired design elements:

Cabinetry/millwork. The Gothic arch design is used primarily for cabinet doors and moldings, both with glass and solid fronts. The trefoil and quatrefoil along with the linen-fold motif also are popular elements for cabinetry and millwork. Oak is the traditional wood, but others of a similar tone are used.

FIGURE 5.5 Gothic arch application in cabinetry door
Courtesy of Wood-Mode Fine Custom Cabinetry

Hardware/fixtures. Ironwork, some burnished silver and bronze, but also wooden knobs are used.

Countertops. Countertops are made of marble, limestone, wood, ceramic tile, and slate as well as laminates, solid surfacing, and engineered stone that simulate natural materials.

Floors. The common materials for floors are any of the natural stones, ceramic tile that simulates any of the stones, and wood planks.

Walls. Walls that are wood paneling or plaster are common.

Ceilings and lighting. Plaster with wood beams or coffers, or solid, carved wood paneling are common. Metal (iron or brass) and glass lighting fixtures, including wall sconces featuring typical Gothic motifs, especially the Gothic arch, or trefoil design, are used.

Colors. Neutrals are popular, especially wood tones and white. Rich versions of red, green, blue, and yellow are popular as accents.

Representative motifs. Gothic arch, trefoil, quatrefoil, linenfold, strapwork carving, colored stained glass windows, and rose windows are popular.

Fabrics. Tapestry weavings, leather, textured linens or cottons, and velvet are used.

Accents/accessories. Tapestries, pewter and silver holloware, iron, and brushed brass metals are popular.

Associated styles. All the Renaissance styles, English Tudor and Jacobean, eighteenth-century Chippendale Gothick, seventeenth-century English and American country styles, Victorian Gothic Revival, Postmodern.

FIGURE 5.6 Gothic arch application in kitchen cabinetry
Courtesy of Wood-Mode Fine Custom Cabinetry

RENAISSANCE

The fifteenth century rediscovery (or rebirth) of ancient Classicism was associated with the rise of cultural sophistication and patronage of the arts, beginning in Florence, Italy. Architecturally, it is associated with the use and renewed interpretation of the Classical orders and motifs in a more elaborate way. This influence spread to the rest of Europe, each region with its own individual design interpretation, primarily in what is now modern-day France, Spain, and England, during the sixteenth and seventeenth centuries. From there it eventually spread to the rest of the world, including North America in the seventeenth century. By the beginning of the eighteenth century, Renaissance styles were replaced by Rococo and later the Neoclassic styles. Rulers and other nobility who lured the skilled Italian craftsmen to their own countries aided the spread of the Renaissance design influence. The French Renaissance was probably the closest interpretation to the Italian, given the close proximity and religious and marital ties of nobility; it is often difficult to differentiate the French Renaissance from the Italian. In many areas of France, Gothic motifs appeared along with those of the Renaissance, often on the same piece of furniture. Spain closely followed the Italian Renaissance designs but also incorporated some of the Islamic and more geometric motifs brought by the Moors. Wrought iron and other metals were used more frequently in Spain, given the lack of abundant forests and wood supply. In England, the Renaissance was called the Tudor or Elizabethan style. It infused some of the Gothic motifs along with Classical ones from Italy, using and emphasizing carved oak.

Renaissance-Inspired Kitchens and Bathrooms

Authentic reproductions of the kitchens and bathrooms of the Renaissance are not sought by today's clients. Instead, they are looking for the look and feeling of the period with all the modern amenities. In the late nineteenth and early twentieth centuries there was a renewed interest in the United States in Renaissance villas and palaces from all over Europe; the wealthy in particular sought to re-create them in the United States. These various Renaissance design elements were incorporated in the interiors as well, including the kitchen and bathroom, which were gradually moving indoors and were more a part of the interior of these larger homes. During the 1960s and 1970s, much of the influence of the Renaissance was reinterpreted (and renamed) as Mediterranean (a combination of Italian and Spanish Renaissance motifs and materials) in contemporary homes. In Figure 5.7 the combination of Italian and Spanish Renaissance design elements is seen in this contemporary kitchen. An English country, more casual version evolved based on the English Renaissance design influences (see Figure 5.8). Since the early 2000s a Tuscan interpretation gained popularity, based primarily on the Italian Renaissance (see Figure 5.9).

FIGURE 5.7 Mediterranean-style kitchen
Courtesy of Wood-Mode Fine Custom Cabinetry

FIGURE 5.8 English country-style Renaissance influenced kitchen
Courtesy of Rutt Hand Crafted Cabinetry
Photo by Don Pearse Photography

Renaissance-inspired design elements:

Cabinetry/millwork. Classical straight lines are common, as are elaborate classical moldings, often with foliage. Medium and dark toned or stained wood such as walnut, possibly distressed cabinetry, moldings, and millwork, are used.

Hardware/fixtures. Ironwork is used primarily, both for hardware and fixtures. Both brushed and shiny metals (brass and pewter) with classical shapes also are used.

Countertops. Marble, limestone, slate, dark-stained wood, laminates, solid surfacing, engineered stone that simulate natural materials, ceramic tile, and decorative mosaics are used.

Floors. Natural stones, like those used on countertops along with ceramic tile or dark stained wood planks are used.

FIGURE 5.9 Tuscan-style kitchen

Design by Tracey Scalzo, CMKBD, Eurotech Cabinetry Inc., Sarasota, FL
Photography by Tom Harper Photography

Walls. Rough plaster, adobe, or ceramic tile is used for walls.

Ceilings and lighting. Plaster or adobe and heavy dark wooden beams are used for ceilings. Metal, especially wrought iron, is used for Spanish and Italian Renaissance–inspired lighting fixtures. For French and English Renaissance lighting, brass or pewter are common. Central fixtures or chandeliers hanging from the ceiling with multiple bulbs, reminiscent of original fixtures that held multiple candles, are used.

Colors. Dark wood tones, off white, and white, rich versions of red, green, blue, and yellow are popular.

Representative motifs. Classical motifs and curves elaborately interpreted are used, as are foliage, cherubs, other human figures, some animals, and a variety of geometric patterns.

Fabrics. Tapestry weavings, tooled leather, velvet, and damask in natural fibers (cotton, linen, wool, and silk) are common.

Accents/accessories. Tapestries, pewter and silver holloware, wrought iron, brushed metals, Renaissance-inspired mosaics and tile, paintings, pottery, and ceramics are all used.

Associated styles. Baroque, country styles, Victorian Renaissance.

BAROQUE PERIOD

In the seventeenth century King Louis XIV of France introduced the Western world to a lavishness in the decorative arts that became the Baroque style, which is an elaboration of the Italian and other Renaissance styles. This style, characterized by more complex, symmetrical, elegant motifs and moldings of mostly classical origins, and required the most skilled craftsmen from throughout Europe to execute them. Materials were more elaborate and reflective, often including gold, silver, and crystal. Although this style influenced architecture and design throughout Europe, the French version is considered the standard that the others in Europe followed. This dominance, influence, and generous support of artisans and craftsmen led to French leadership in design and the decorative arts that continued well into the twentieth century. The English styles of Jacobean, William and Mary, and Queen Anne are their simpler versions of Baroque, as is the early Georgian style of Thomas Chippendale. Because of the elaborateness and complexity of the style, the French Baroque has been copied or adapted less frequently than the English versions.

Baroque-Inspired Kitchens and Bathrooms

Baroque inspiration and influence occasionally are seen in kitchens and bathrooms, primarily in cabinetry, moldings, and accents. Elaborate classically inspired motifs and moldings are characteristic, as are accessories, artwork, or elaborate textiles reminiscent of the times, although they generally are simplified as seen in the kitchen in Figure 5.10, or used more dramatically in separate, smaller spaces, such as the bathroom in Figure 5.11, to suit contemporary homes, lifestyles, and tastes.

FIGURE 5.10 Baroque-influenced kitchen
Design by James E. Howard, CKD, CBD, Glen Alspaugh Co., LLP, St. Louis, MO
Photo by Alise O'Brien Photography

FIGURE 5.11 Baroque-influenced bathroom

Design by Shea Pumarejom, Younique Designs, Helotes, TX
Photo by Casey Dunn

Baroque-inspired design elements:

Cabinetry/millwork. Classical curved lines, elaborate classical moldings, often with abundant foliage, are used. Dark wood or "antiqued" painted light wood cabinetry, moldings, and millwork are common, with accents of gold or silver.

Hardware/fixtures. Brass, shiny, brushed, or aged, is used primarily for cabinet hardware and plumbing fixtures, with elaborate classical and primarily symmetrical curves.

Countertops. Marble and other stones, dark and dark-stained woods, laminates, solid surfacing, engineered stone that simulates natural materials, and decorative tile mosaics are used.

Floors. Marble and wood in intricate patterns as well as limestone are used.

Walls: Elaborately carved wood paneling, plaster that is painted and mirrored walls are common.

Ceilings and lighting. Plaster and wood beamed ceilings are used. For lighting, elaborate, multi-armed brass, pewter, silver, or iron fixtures, often with glass pendants, are common.

Colors. Dark wood tones and white, intense versions of red, green, blue, and yellow, gold, and silver metallic tones are found.

Representative motifs. Classical and curvilinear motifs, more elaborately interpreted, foliage, cherubs, and other human figures are common.

Fabrics. Tapestry weavings, silk velvets, damasks, and brocades are used.

Accents/accessories. Tapestries; gold, brass, and silver holloware; mosaics; paintings; and French and Chinese porcelains are used.

Associated styles. Renaissance, Rococo, French provincial, eighteenth-century Georgian, Chinese

ROCOCO AND FRENCH PROVINCIAL/COUNTRY PERIODS

The Rococo style developed in France as the heaviness and elaborateness of the Baroque was waning in the early eighteenth century. Rococo (meaning "rocks and shells" in French) was a style based on nature and natural elements, a departure from the classical influence of the Renaissance and Baroque. Some might call it whimsical, even ethereal, and it is usually asymmetrical, with a dominance of free-flowing gentle curves, typically lighter in scale and color, smaller in size, and less grand than the previous Baroque. The Rococo style of the French became popular throughout Europe, adapted with various regional and cultural interpretations. Among the more common is the English interpretation (known as French or Rococo Chippendale) of Thomas Chippendale. Late in the nineteenth century, French Rococo was also an inspiration for selected French Art Nouveau designers.

The curves and motifs of the Rococo style were the inspiration for a majority of the furniture made and used in homes in the French provinces beginning in the late seventeenth century, popularly known as French provincial or French country. This style is reflective of homes dotting the French villages and countryside, which were furnished by prosperous merchants and farmers with furnishings and room settings initially inspired by the Parisian court's high style but were simplified and made much less pretentious by regional, less skilled workmen. However, French country rooms can be sophisticated and include a great deal of detail. This style remains popular and is in use at the present time, not only in France but worldwide.

These rooms—like many European country settings—have a sense of evolving. They are a collection of patterns, colors, and materials that please the occupants, having been gathered by the family over time. The rooms are relatively light in color and typically have a feminine sense, with curved lines dominating. Simple lines and small-scale furniture are common in a peasant French atmosphere; more complex arrangements work well in more refined, formal rooms.

FIGURE 5.12 Rococo/ French provincial–inspired kitchen
Design by Mark T. White, CKD, CBD, Kitchen Encounters, Annapolis, MD
Photo by Phoenix Photographic

Rococo/French Provincial–Inspired Kitchens and Bathrooms

When the Rococo is a design influence in kitchens and bathrooms today, it is most often in the simplified form of the French Provincial or French country. The motifs are similar, the smaller scale and the simpler versions are more suitable to contemporary taste and interiors, yet they still create an ambiance of the French countryside (see Figures 5.12 and 5.13).

Rococo/French provincial–inspired design elements:

Cabinetry/millwork. Walnut, pine, cherry, and a variety of fruitwoods are used in natural and light-painted finishes with some aging, distressing, or artistic enhancement. Glass or wire mesh door inserts are also used. Generally light-colored surfaces are also appropriate in French country style. Mixing colors and wood finishes in an unfitted cabinet style environment reflects the casual style of a French home in the provinces.

Hardware/fixtures. Bronze, copper, iron, or pewter is used. Hammered surfaces are acceptable but polished are more historically accurate. Oversized hardware—long metal hinges—and fanciful hand-wrought details, including elaborate lighting fixtures, are common.

FIGURE 5.13 Rococo/French provincial–inspired bathroom
Courtesy of Wood-Mode Fine Custom Cabinetry

Countertops. Solid surface, quartz, natural or manmade marble, natural stone, ceramic tile, or laminate countertops with detailed edges can all be used effectively. Solid surface counters may feature delicate tile inlays or gently sculptured edge treatments. Ceramic tile that is smooth in texture with matching grout colors is used on counter or splash areas. Decorative laminate counters combine well with wood or faux wood front edges and ceramic tile (could be decorative, painted tile) backsplash areas.

Floors. Heavy, rustic materials, such as brick, limestone, or terra cotta quarry tiles, are common, as are hardwood parquet or plank patterns in reproduction or natural products.

Walls. Painted plaster walls, toile de Jouy, or floral wallcovering, either fabric or wallpaper with small patterns, are typical. Delicate crown moldings and beaded baseboards are also used. Faux-finished decorative treatments that simulate aged wood finishes are also common.

Ceilings and lighting. Plaster with boxed wood beams finished to match or to contrast with cabinets or ceiling finish, beaded or random wood plank ceilings reflect the rustic sense of a French country setting. Multi-armed chandeliers in rustic, antiqued, or tole-painted metal with candelabra bulbs are typical for lighting fixtures.

Colors. Country French rooms often contrast warm and cool color groupings. Combinations of blue and yellow, red and yellow, or red and green are commonly used. For example, wood tones can be warm with cooler accessory colors or the reverse. Pastels are also appropriate in a French setting, as are the more vibrant colors and patterns seen in the French patterned fabrics from the south of France.

Representative motifs. Pastoral scenes, nature, animals (roosters in particular), foliage motifs, and small prints (i.e., floral, olives) are common.

Fabrics. Cottons, linens, primarily, in small prints, scenics, and toile de Jouy are used.

Accents/Accessories. Common are metals, fine porcelain pieces called French faience, as well as country ceramics, curved mullion doors with beveled glass, metal wire mesh, and delicately patterned fabrics associated with the South of France. Lace fabric on shelves inside cabinets with glass doors is typical. A mantel hood area or a fireplace in the kitchen can be included. Tall and narrow large windows with rectangular hardware and a deep sill created in reality or as a visual effect are common.

Accent furniture pieces. The formality (or informality) of the room can be enhanced by suggesting the typical regional pieces. Provincial furniture was made by skilled chair and cabinetmakers from larger cities throughout France. French country furniture— the more rustic pieces—was made for farmhouses in Provence and Normandy, hunting lodges in Burgundy, and the modest cottages in the Ile de France. The forms of these pieces usually mirrored Parisian styles but lacked excess carving and ornamentation.

Associated styles. Baroque, seventeenth- and eighteenth-century English and American country, Biedermeier.

GEORGIAN PERIOD

At the beginning of the seventeenth century, the European (primarily English) influences spread to North America, with the early Puritans arriving in New England and gentlemen farmers in Jamestown, Virginia. They brought a few treasured family objects and a sense of style from their European homes that were then adapted or copied by local craftsmen with local materials. Although homes were initially quite rugged, the furnishings within typically demonstrated the style and status of the generally prosperous owners. It was not until the eighteenth century that the more elaborate and formal styles were introduced in North America. As the United States became more prosperous and money was more available, then more formal American styles evolved and became common. These styles, characterized by ornamentation reflecting what was going on in Europe at the same time, typically were simpler, using abundant local hardwoods and produced by local craftsmen. Influences came from the English styles, the late Jacobean, William and Mary, Queen Anne, and Georgian predominated throughout the eighteenth century and well into the nineteenth and twentieth centuries. These styles are identified by a variety of terms, which can be confusing to designers and clients. Some of these terms include colonial (early colonial during the seventeenth century, late colonial in the eighteenth century), as during most of this time the United States was an English colony; Early American (usually referring to prior to the Revolutionary War); American traditional (generally both the seventeenth and eighteenth centuries); or even the broad term traditional (usually any style prior to the nineteenth century). Precise definitions are difficult to come by and not all sources agree on a single one, adding to the confusion.

Georgian-Inspired Kitchens and Bathrooms

The Georgian style developed under the kings George (I, II, III, and IV) of England (ca. 1714–1810) and spread to North America with the colonists. Work by designers such as Chippendale, Hepplewhite, and Sheraton characterized the Georgian style at its best. Georgian is a formal style with classical ties, so symmetry in placement of fixtures and cabinetry is important. Within these designs, molding details resulting in grand friezes, elaborate cornices, pillars, and pilasters

FIGURE 5.14 Georgian-inspired kitchen
Design by Nicholas Geragi, CKD, CBD, codesigner Damani King, Klaff's Inc, Norwalk, CT

are important. Classical designs such as dentil, egg and dart, and Greek key are seen in many of the molding details. Carved corbels, brackets and appliqués, or inlays of acanthus leaf and leafy garlands are also incorporated. The use of moldings and wood paneling is a key element to this style. The scalloped shell motif is seen in furniture detailing. Delicate curves and soft lines are also trademarks. A formal look and quality craftsmanship are hallmarks of this more refined interior, including kitchens and bathrooms (see Figures 5.14 and 5.15).

Georgian-inspired design elements:

> **Cabinetry/millwork.** Use mahogany, walnut, cherry, and maple and stile-and-rail doors with solid raised panels or flat panel doors with applied square molding and detailed panel edging. Painted light cabinet finishes or lightly glazed painted finishes reflect the wood-work of the time.

> **Hardware/fixtures.** Brass, antique brass, copper, or pewter are appropriate in classically inspired curved designs.

> **Countertops.** Wood and wood-edged countertops or solid surface material with formal, routed edges are used. Hand-painted tiles, granite or marble both work well in these more traditional and formal rooms.

FIGURE 5.15 Georgian-inspired bathroom
Design by Jeannie Fulton, CKD, CBD, Ulrich Inc., Ridgewood, NJ

FIGURE 5.16 American country/colonial–inspired kitchen
Courtesy of The Corsi Group, Inc. Robert Millman Photography

Floors. Plank or parquet wood (or simulated wood) flooring, stone or ceramic tile, oriental area rugs, hall runners, and area carpets work in both kitchens and bathrooms.

Walls. Use painted, wood paneled walls, with wood wainscoting. Small patterned wallcoverings such as toile, floral, or Oriental patterns are common.

Ceilings and lighting. Use plaster, plain, textured, or carved with crown molding for the ceiling. Traditional, eighteenth-century candelabra-shaped chandeliers and wall sconces in shiny brass or pewter with crystal are typical lighting fixtures.

Colors. Black (Asian influence), white, red, green, blue; intense colors are used. Tints and tones of these colors are also used.

Representative motifs. Classically inspired motifs, such as garlands, urns, and Greek and Roman columns, are common.

Fabrics. Use tapestry, needlework such as crewel embroideries, velvet, damask, brocades, moiré chintz, and satins.

Accents/accessories. Utilize gold, silver, brass, or antique brass metals as well as fine French, English, or Chinese porcelains. Furniture pieces of the period add authenticity.

Associated styles. Neoclassic, Baroque, Chinese, and French Rococo.

AMERICAN COUNTRY (OR RUSTIC) STYLES

Also occurring during the seventeenth through the nineteenth centuries, away from the large eastern cities as the United States expanded westward, were simpler, more rustic, country styles of homes and furnishings, reflecting the diversity of cultural and religious design influences that were prevalent in the United States. The influence was predominantly English at first, called by a variety of names; three of the more common ones were country, colonial, and traditional. Other influences that emerged during the eighteenth century were the German influence in Pennsylvania, known popularly as Pennsylvania Dutch; the Dutch influence in New York and Delaware, known as American Dutch; the religious sect influence of the Shakers in the midwest and northeastern United States; and the Spanish Mission style reflected in the missions that were established in California and the southwest. Of these, the English-influenced colonial, Shaker, and the Spanish Mission styles have been the most adapted in contemporary interiors, including kitchens to a greater degree than bathrooms.

American Country/American Colonial–Inspired Kitchens and Bathrooms

The American country style of the seventeenth and early eighteenth centuries is based on early American colonial influences in New England and along the East Coast that came primarily from England. Handcrafted simplicity is the hallmark of this style: turned wood posts, straight lines, square or rectangular shapes. This style features sturdy, rugged, and crudely constructed elements. The pineapple motif, a symbol of hospitality, is often used in hammered metal accents, carved plaster, or stenciling patterns. Because of the rustic details, country styles are primarily an informal and casual setting. The typical colonial (or country) home combined rustic handmade furnishings created in the New World, with perhaps an occasional formal piece the family brought with them from Europe. The early colonists were proud of their possessions and displayed them. Open shelving, rough-hewn materials, and painted cabinetry are commonly seen in these colonial-style homes (see Figures 5.16 and 5.17).

American country/American colonial design elements:

Cabinetry/millwork. Maple, pine, oak, birch, cherry, and fruitwoods in natural or light finishes are common. Finish cabinets, painted in solid colors, or featuring faux finishes on the woodwork are used as well. Stile-and-rail flat panel doors, butted board doors, or doors that include beaded board center panels are appropriate. Because of the rustic nature of this period, the door styling is simple. A built-in corner cupboard is also

FIGURE 5.17 American country/colonial–inspired bathroom
Courtesy of Wood-Mode Fine Custom Cabinetry

appropriate, as is a butcher-block table or island or sideboard type of cabinet accent piece. For a country look, the cabinetry should have more of a furniture or freestanding appearance rather than the totally integrated look found in contemporary kitchens and bathrooms.

Hardware/fixtures. Use decorative brass with ceramic inlays, wrought iron, copper, oil-rubbed bronze, antique brass, or pewter for hardware and plumbing fixtures.

Countertops. Use tile, square-edged solid surface materials, wood-trimmed laminate (that simulate a natural material), wood, natural granite, slate, or soapstone.

Floors. Use natural, rugged materials (real or simulated), such as wood plank, brick, or rustic stone or ceramic tile.

Walls. Use plaster walls, painted white or off-white, natural stone, brick, beaded-board, stenciled patterns either directly on the wall or in a wallpaper or wainscoting.

Ceilings and lighting. Use plaster for ceilings, painted white or off-white with hand-hewn wood beams or solid wood. For lighting, simple rustic fixtures (reminiscent of candle holders) in wrought iron, pewter, or brushed gold-colored metal work well.

Colors. Extensive use of the primary and secondary colors—red, blue, yellow, green, orange, and purple—reflect original natural dye colors. Alternatively, use "antiqued" or muted tones so the colors appear as if they are old and were applied years ago.

FIGURE 5.18 Kitchen cabinetry with open shelving and simple cabinetry influenced by the Shaker style

Design by Carol Swanson-Petterson, CKD, KB Cabinets, Millbrae, CA
Photo by Daniel Cronin

Representative motifs. Classically inspired motifs, foliage (fruits, flowers, vines), pineapple, tree of life, and animals are common.

Fabrics. Use tapestry, needlework such as crewel embroideries, linen block, or stencil linen and cotton prints, leather. Small patterns that reflect stenciled designs or the hand-woven nature of the textiles from this period are also appropriate.

Accents/accessories. Use wrought iron and pewter, simple pottery, handmade woven rag or braided rugs.

Associated styles. Renaissance, English Tudor and Jacobean, French Provincial, other country styles, Gothic.

Shaker–Inspired Kitchens and Bathrooms

"Shaker styling" is a term used to define a woodworking styling that is well executed but simple in detail that is attributed to the craftspeople of the Shaker (a religious sect) villages located primarily in the northeastern and midwestern United States from the late eighteenth through the nineteenth centuries. The last Shaker village closed in the early twentieth century,

FIGURE 5.19 Bathroom vanity storage cabinetry influenced by the Shaker style
Design by Scott and Sandra Gjesdahl, Bristol Design and Construction, Kirkland, WA

with only a few members remaining after that. However, their objects and designs continue to be manufactured and used today.

The Shakers believed an important part of celebrating God was to always be busy and active in worthwhile tasks and to demand the best of oneself in the way one lived as well as in the products one created. They are credited with many developments that are in use in interiors today. The Shaker concept of built-in cabinetry for efficient storage has contributed greatly to the design of cabinets used not only in kitchens and bathrooms, but throughout the home. The Shakers' homes were really dormitories—with men living in one (or on one side) and women in the other—and were designed with multifunctional rooms. Chairs hung on pegs when not in use and built-in cupboards lined the walls, freeing up floor space for other activities.

The design elements used by the Shakers focused on simplicity of detail and refinement of craftsmanship (some say the beginnings of contemporary design), as well as providing necessary storage in a small space, and thus lend themselves to both kitchen and bathroom design in almost any interior or historical architectural style today, as seen in Figures 5.18 and 5.19.

Shaker-inspired design elements:

Cabinetry/millwork. Use stile-and-rail recessed panel doors with a plain inset, or flat panel doors with lip construction; simple outside edge detail. Cherry and maple woods

FIGURE 5.20 Spanish Mission–inspired kitchen
Design by Cheryl-Hamilton-Gray, CKD, Hamilton-Gray Design Inc., Carlsbad, CA
Photo by Brandon Barre

(or stained those tones) are used extensively. Some figured wood, such as bird's-eye maple or tiger maple, is used as well. Use waxed or oiled warm-medium range wood tones. Occasionally, some of the woodwork, such as the window frames, peg rail, skirting, cabinetry, or beaded board wall system, would be painted one of the typical Shaker colors, or white, detailed below. Open shelving for dish storage or display of typical Shaker-style accessories (boxes, pottery, glass) was also used.

Hardware/fixtures. Use plain round wooden knob cabinet and drawer pulls, wood pegs for wall hanging systems. Use simple or hand-forged metal, usually with brushed or matte finishes with simple lines or geometric curves.

Countertops. Use square-edged solid surfaces, wood, slate, soapstone, granite, and limestone in a solid, rather than any obvious pattern.

Floors. Typically, floors are varnished timber or wood, occasionally they are stone. Simple woven wool or rag rugs were laid on top of these hard surface floors.

Walls. For walls, paint in solid earth tones or off-white. Typically, tall beaded board wainscoting in cherry or maple was used with pegs.

Ceilings and lighting. Use plain plaster ceilings, painted white or off-white. Wood beams could also be used. For lighting, use simple rectilinear fixtures in pewter or plain glass with no added decoration or ornamentation.

Colors. Shaker dwellings were typically white plaster, against which a set range of mostly muted colors was used for both paint and textiles. The distinctive color palette made use of the dyes and pigments from the clays and plants around them, ranging from pinky tones and terra cotta earth shades, through yellow ochre and olive green, to greenish and denim blues.

Representative motifs. Use simple straight lines, stripes or check patterns, incorporating only one or two colors. Use of elaborate, multicolored, decorative patterns was not encouraged.

Fabrics. Fabrics were linen, cotton, or wool, hand-woven and frequently plain, textured, stripes, or checks as the Shakers avoided the use of more decorative or elaborate patterns.

Accents/accessories. Simple earth-toned pottery and glass, as well as round or oval wooden boxes in either wood tones or painted a typical earth-tone color also are used.

Associated styles. American country/colonial, Swedish country, Scandinavian modern, Arts and Crafts, Japanese, Italian/European modern, Bauhaus, postmodern.

Spanish Mission–Inspired Kitchens and Bathrooms

The Spanish Mission styling is a refined country style, using metals extensively and geometric patterns in tile and stone, rough, often dark woodwork, and dark-beamed ceilings based primarily on the Spanish Renaissance style. Patterns in materials (such as tiles) are also influenced by the Moorish design aesthetic brought from Spain by colonists to Mexico and then reinterpreted by settlers in the American southwest and California, now adapted today in kitchens and bathrooms (see Figures 5.20 and 5.21).

FIGURE 5.21 Spanish Mission–inspired master bathroom
Design by Cheryl Hamilton-Gray, CKD, Hamilton-Gray Design Inc., Carlsbad, CA
Photo by Scott McKay

Spanish Mission–inspired design elements:

Cabinetry/millwork. Use walnut, pine, or oak. Simple cabinet detailing is common: for example, doors with turned posts; stile-and-rail doors with curved or square tops; plank door styles, or square raised or recessed panel. Cabinet finishes can be whitewash, pickled, natural, distressed, or painted dark or light tones. Hand-carved details in simple naturalistic motifs accentuate the space.

Hardware/Fixtures. Rustic, hand-forged metals, such as wrought iron, copper, and pewter, and wood are appropriate.

Countertops. They are natural and heavy in appearance and texture, and generally matte in finish. Wood, slate, soapstone, granite, and ceramic tile are also appropriate materials.

Floors. Use random-patterned flagstone, slate, large adobelike tile (glazed or unglazed), or wide random-plank distressed wood floors.

Walls. Use a simple often almost whitewash, rough or adobe finish, with ceramic tile as a backsplash.

Ceilings and lighting. Use white or soft light neutral color or plaster, accented with dark, rough, heavy wood beams. The most common lighting fixtures are elaborately forged wrought iron, both as multi-candled chandeliers and wall sconces.

Colors. White, off-white or neutral base color with warm, sun-baked earth-toned color accents are common; grayed tones as well as intense primary and secondary colors, especially red, are also appropriate accents.

Representative motifs. Naturalistic plants and animals, Renaissance-inspired classical motifs, geometric, Gothic, and Moorish geometric motifs are used.

Fabrics. Use leather, hand-woven textured linens or wools, velvet, Native American textiles, and European tapestries.

Accents/accessories. Reproduction and antique baskets, pottery, western and landscape paintings, and horticultural prints all have a sense of the Spanish Mission. Use wrought iron and pounded brass metals, succulent and cacti greenery, nubby area carpets in solid colors or with Navajo Indian patterns, leather or dark Spanish wood furniture, and heavy pottery.

Associated styles. Renaissance (Spanish in particular but also Italian), Arts and Crafts, Gothic.

NEOCLASSIC STYLES

The Neoclassic or new classic styles from the end of the eighteenth and early nineteenth centuries developed primarily as a result of the unearthing of the ruins of Pompeii and Herculaneum (covered for centuries by the ash from the eruption of Mt. Vesuvius) south of Naples, Italy, in the mid-1700s. Young architects from throughout Europe (predominantly men) traveled there (as part of their "grand tour" experience) to see, draw, and eventually copy the architectural elements and designs they found for the exteriors, interiors, and furnishings of royalty and the prosperous estate owners of their respective countries.

Several variations of the Neoclassic style emerged as a result of the discoveries. The styles were primarily in France (Louis XVI and Directoire) and England (Robert Adam), which in turn influenced design and designers/cabinetmakers throughout Europe and eventually North America. The styles evolved in the nineteenth-century, as English Regency in England. Napoleon introduced it as the French Empire style in France, also including some of the Egyptian motifs. These Neoclassic styles eventually developed into the somewhat simpler Swedish Neoclassic in Scandinavia, and a more common man's version typified as Biedermeier in Austria and Germany. These Neoclassic influences spread to the Americas from the later part of the eighteenth into the early nineteenth century with the American Federal and Empire styles and Greek Revival architecture, which developed in the early nineteenth century as the country grew and prospered. These are most notably rather nonspecific late eighteenth-century versions, incorporating both French and English elements. Because the variations were so similar, it is often difficult to distinguish between them, so the umbrella term "Neoclassic" is often used to name this style.

Neoclassic-Inspired Kitchens and Bathrooms

Today, because of the Classical origins and close adherence to the elements and principles of design, the Neoclassic influence continues to be incorporated in both kitchens and bathrooms, along with other aspects of the exterior and interior architecture and design. The Neoclassic influence takes several forms when used in interiors, including kitchens and bathrooms, as there are several style interpretations. Probably the most commonly used of these Neoclassic styles currently is a version that is difficult to distinguish specifically (often simply called Neoclassic for this reason) that incorporates aspects of the French Louis XVI and Directoire; the English cabinetmakers Robert Adam, George Hepplewhite, and Thomas Sheraton; and the Scottish-American Duncan Phyfe. They use similar elements (rectangles, symmetry, pilasters), colors (pale yellow, green, peach, white), and motifs (classical moldings, geometric shapes) as interpreted in a Neoclassical-inspired kitchen and bathroom (see Figures 5.22 and 5.23). A similar interpretation of the Neoclassic style is found in the Swedish/

FIGURE 5.22 Neoclassic-inspired kitchen
Courtesy of Sub-Zero Wolf, Design by Ellen Cheever, CMKBD, ASID, Ellen Cheever & Associates, Wilmington, DE

FIGURE 5.23 Neoclassic-inspired bathroom

Design by Leslie Lamarre, CKD, CID, CGBP, codesigner Erika Shjeflo, CID, TRG Architects, Burlingame, CA
Bernard Andre Photography

Scandinavian versions (see Figures 5.24 and 5.25), which additionally uses subtle gray or blue and white. The German/Austrian Biedermeier is another Neoclassic style that has its own unique characteristics: light fruitwood wood tones with touches of black and occasionally a bright primary color, distinguishing it from the other Neoclassic styles (see Figures 5.26 and 5.27). The English Regency and French Empire, as well as the American Federal and Empire, are used less often in kitchen and bathroom design and are difficult to distinguish from the broad Neoclassic style.

Neoclassic-inspired design elements:

The Neoclassic style is most often perceived as formal, predominantly symmetrical, dignified, and classical because of geometric patterns and detailing, such as the Greek key seen throughout this type of space.

> **Cabinetry/millwork.** Use mahogany, walnut, or cherry wood. Use inset doors with classic Greek key molding or other intricate, applied classical molding. Stile-and-rail doors with curved raised panels or detailed glass and muntin or mullion cabinet doors are common, with classic white or off-white, or other pale color finishes.

> **Hardware/fixtures.** Formal hardware is used in polished brass or brushed pewter or other intricate metalwork with classically inspired curves.

FIGURE 5.24 Swedish/Scandinavian Neoclassic-inspired kitchen
Courtesy of Kohler Company

Countertops. Use laminate or solid surface countertops that simulate a natural material, with detailed edges, or natural stones in a polished finish. Delicate and patterned tiles can be used as accents.

Floors.. Wood parquet patterns, simple square vinyl, ceramic, or stone tiles (usually black and white) are common.

Walls. Plaster or paneled walls, often with wainscoting, either wood toned or painted a typical color, elaborate door and window moldings are used.

Ceilings and lighting. Plaster ceilings with crown moldings are common. For lighting, pewter or brass traditional candelabra fixtures are used.

Colors. Red, blue, yellow, green, primarily as muted pastels, along with white, gray, and black are used.

Representative motifs. Greek and Roman classically inspired motifs, stripes, ribbons, classical medallions, and garlands are common.

Fabrics. Satin, damask, brocade, velvet, moiré, tapestry, petit points, and patterned silks from the Far East are used.

Accents/accessories. Use brass and gold metals to trim countertops, fine Chinese porcelains, and others from the Far East.

Associated styles. Georgian, Biedermeier, all other Classic and Neoclassic styles, postmodern.

FIGURE 5.25 Swedish/Scandinavian Neoclassic-inspired bathroom
Courtesy of Kohler Company

Swedish Neoclassic

The long, dark northern winter nights have led many Swedish (and other Scandinavian) interiors to feature lighter pastel colors and simpler details. Readily available materials in the Scandinavian environment are used instead of costly and rare ones that need to be imported. Because the region is heavily forested, interiors feature simple woods and handmade materials.

Swedish Neoclassic-inspired design elements:

Cabinetry/millwork. Pine, birch, beech, and other tightly grained and light colored woods are appropriate. Painted or pale, limed finishes, white, or natural finishes on wood are used. An uncluttered look is a hallmark of Swedish styling, with a focus on functional space and storage. Open shelving mixed with dressers, sideboards, and other furniture pieces converted to kitchen use, are appropriate. Simple frame and recess panel door styles with delicate, simple moldings based on Classical motifs are used.

Hardware/fixtures. Simplicity, symmetry, and usefulness are hallmarks, in porcelain, wood, or pewter.

Countertops. Wood is the most realistic; wood-grained laminate, rustic stone, or tile is also appropriate. A quartz or similar material as a solid would be an appropriate choice.

FIGURE 5.26 Biedermeier-inspired kitchen
Courtesy of GE Appliances

Floors. Wood floors that are scrubbed, lime-washed, or finished with a gray tone are used with rag rugs and runners in red, gray, cream, or pale blue.

Walls. Stenciling, solid and faux painting may be used on the soft tone-on-tone pastel finishes.

Ceilings and lighting. Use simple painted ceilings in pastel shades. For lighting, use simple pewter, chrome or nickel fixtures in a brushed finish with a translucent glass reflector.

Colors. White, gray, blue, pale green, yellow, red, and ecru are very typical, with touches of brown or bottle green also used.

Representative motifs. Simple, classically inspired shapes and motifs, stripes, ribbons, classical medallions, and garlands are common.

Fabrics. Use cottons, linens, and wools. Patterns are used sparingly; they are usually nubby textures, woven checks and stripes, or delicate and subtle floral prints.

Accents/Accessories. Blue and white ceramics, simple metal and wood objects, both natural and painted, are used.

Associated styles. English, French, and American Neoclassic styles, Biedermeier, Bauhaus, Art Deco, Shaker, Scandinavian modern, midcentury modern, postmodern.

FIGURE 5.27 Biedermeier-inspired bathroom
Design by Gay Fly, Gay Fly Designer Kitchens & Baths, Galveston, TX

Biedermeier

The German/Austrian version of the Neoclassic is called Biedermeier. It flourished in Europe from 1820 to about the middle of the1850s, influenced by the French Empire, English Regency, and French Directoire styles. It has enjoyed recent and continued popularity because of its simplicity, the warm lighter-toned fruitwoods and cherry woods used with contrasting black detailing, which makes it an interesting element in a contemporary home. A side note: The name is not that of a famous designer or architect. It grew out of a cartoon character named "Papa Biedermeier" (in German meaning "simple" and Meier, a common German surname). The style is a simplified classically based style designed specifically for the middle class, yet uses sophisticated geometric and classical forms. Of importance is the strong contrast between dark and pale woods, black, and gilded accents, which are some of its hallmarks.

Biedermeier-inspired design elements:

Cabinetry/millwork. Use clear light to medium colored wood with simple lines such as in maple, beech, ash, or cherry, often with a narrow beaded inset panel. The bead may be finished black or touch of gold, as might other moldings and hardware selections. The moldings are simple in nature and have flowing classical lines.

Hardware/fixtures. Use traditional, classically inspired style with linear detailing. Brass, bronze, black, or other gold colored metal surfaces are common.

Countertops. Use granite, engineered stone, or solid laminate in dark solid or subtly textured colors, such as black or variations of gray.

Floors. Use wood strip floors in medium fruitwood tones bordered with a darker wood. Also possible are light toned limestone, marble, or similar tile floors.

Walls. Use a plain or vertical patterned wallcovering (stripes are typical), textured faux, geometric patterned finishes, and a simple border, such as the wave or Greek key motif.

Ceilings and lighting. Use painted light (white or off-white), relatively simple ceilings. Brass or black metal, classical light fixtures are common.

Colors. Backdrop colors used are subtle beiges, creams, reds, vibrant yellows, blues, soft grays, aquamarine, sandstone, and parchment with black and gilt accents.

Representative motifs. Simple, classically inspired motifs include stripes, geometric patterns, Greek key, wave, and lozenges (flat diamond motifs).

Fabrics. Use geometric prints and stripes, cotton, linen, wool, solid velvets, leather, horsehair fabric, and woven nubby textures.

Accents/accessories. Simple, classically inspired metals and ceramics are used.

Associated styles. English, French, and American Neoclassic styles, Arts and Crafts, Art Deco, Shaker, Scandinavian modern.

VICTORIAN PERIOD AND THE RISE OF INDUSTRIALIZATION

Shortly after the beginning of the nineteenth century, the nature and style of architecture in the Western world underwent an abrupt change due to the effect of the Industrial Revolution and machine manufacturing, the rise of a middle class, as well as an increase in the extremely wealthy population, especially in America. This was reflected, for example, in the increased size of houses and the accumulation of "things." The first large mansions were ways of showing prosperity, wealth, and status, as well as to showcase accumulated possessions. As a result, many looked to the models of castles, villas, chateaus, and palaces in Europe for design inspiration and reinterpretation. The Victorian versions of Gothic, Renaissance, Italianate, and Romanesque styles developed during this century. Also as a result of industrialization, workers, their jobs, and their families moved from the rural countryside to cities, creating urban housing that was often small and cramped. Homes, and therefore lives, changed. New materials and technology became available through the Industrial Revolution, and new demands were placed on buildings and their interiors. By the end of the nineteenth century, plumbing started to move indoors, along with food preparation, creating design and building challenges and changes.

The Victorian era is named after Queen Victoria of England and coincides with the beginning of the Industrial Revolution. Queen Victoria was an enthusiastic amateur artist and decorator, personally designing her palace at Balmoral using light wood tones, pale blue and green accents, and plenty of glass to let the light in—not what most associate with the Victorian style. The Victorian style typically seen in interiors today is extremely detailed because of the preponderance of machine-made woodworking, dark and somber in color tones with heavy wood grains. Reinterpreted historical motifs, such as stylized floral patterns, filigree, Gothic lancet-arched windows, and leaded glass panes, create the intricately detailed themes popular in Victorian interiors.

Victorian-Inspired Kitchens and Bathrooms

It was during the Victorian era that kitchens and bathrooms as we know them today moved indoors to become part of the main house rather than as separate exterior facilities. This was primarily due to technological advances that allowed plumbing to gradually be moved indoors, allowing for greater convenience and improved sanitation in both kitchens and

FIGURE 5.28 Victorian-style kitchen

Courtesy of Kohler Company

bathrooms. In general, function of the space, rather than design or aesthetic considerations, was the primary concern. These were work and private spaces, generally not meant for guests or socializing, or designed to show status or impress others. In contemporary kitchens and bathrooms in Victorian-style homes, the design motifs and materials, along with the "vintage" style of cabinetry, fixtures, and appliances available today, give the Victorian feeling to the spaces (see Figures 5.28 and 5.29).

Victorian-inspired design elements:

Cabinetry/millwork. Use heavy dark woods such as mahogany, blackened oak, black walnut, satinwood, or rosewood. Painted cabinetry and moldings in a variety of colors are also common. Also use raised panel or beveled glass doors, multiple panel doors, heavily stacked moldings, and hand-carved appliqués or inlays.

Hardware/fixtures. Ornate polished brass, ceramic, or marble inset with inlays are common.

Countertops. Use wood, marble, granite, and ceramic tiles or solid surfacing that simulates natural materials.

Floors. Use patterned floors—in reproduction linoleum and vinyl, or marble, limestone, mosaic tile, or wood strip or parquet patterns.

Walls. Use plaster or imported wallcoverings with Asian or historical themes. Flocked silk damask fabric, anaglypta, lincrusta, and other heavy materials are also used as wall coverings. (Anaglypta and lincrusta are meant to be painted.) Wood or tooled leather wainscot dado paneling that continues down the wall to the baseboard molding is also used. A thick ceiling crown molding was used to hang pictures from so the hardware did not damage the wall covering. A running bond brick or tile backsplash is common.

Ceilings and lighting. As ceilings are typically high, white or other light color that blends with the wall color is an option. While generally plastered, it is not uncommon to use hammered tin or painted anaglypta on the ceiling. Intricate, ornate glass, often colored, and metal light fixtures are used, reminiscent of those from the castles in Europe.

Colors. Typically, very dark, rich colors are used, such as olive green, burgundy, blue, yellow, black, and white. However, lighter, subtle variations, especially pink, are acceptable.

Representative motifs. Formal patterns include Classical and Gothic motifs, plants and foliage, and animals.

Fabrics. Heavy fabrics for window treatments, lace, velvet, brocade, damask, tapestry, needlework, cloth woven from real horsehair are common.

Accents/accessories. Intricately detailed, elaborate furniture and Oriental-type carpets are used. Glass, porcelains, and silver from around the world, especially the Far East, are used.

Associated styles. Gothic, Renaissance, Baroque, Rococo, Chinese.

SUMMARY

Knowing about and being able to apply knowledge to create a historic (or historic-inspired) style to the design of kitchens and bathrooms is important for the designer. Successive design styles build on what has gone on before, yet each has its own unique interpretation and innovations. The designer needs to keep in mind that the aesthetic design of kitchens and bathrooms was not a significant consideration in interior home design until the twentieth century; therefore, much of what guides the use of a historic style in these spaces is based on architectural and interior elements as well as furnishing styles. Occasionally the designer will encounter an existing eighteenth, nineteenth, or twentieth century home or one that is reminiscent of one of those periods where the client would like to use the style and feeling of the architectural style in the interior spaces. The information in this chapter is a necessary foundation to understanding the design of kitchens and bathrooms that eventually emerged in the twentieth century and are discussed in Chapter 6.

FIGURE 5.29 Victorian-influenced bathroom vanity

Courtesy of Kohler Company

REVIEW QUESTIONS

1. Identify the steps involved in creating an historic theme for a kitchen or bathroom project. (See "Establishing a Historic Theme for a Kitchen or Bathroom Project" pages 123–125)

2. Identify styles based on some of the design elements of the classical Greek and/or Roman styles. (See "Ancient/Classical Period" pages 125–129)

3. Identify styles prevalent today that were influenced by elements of the Renaissance. (See "Renaissance" pages 131–133)

4. Identify characteristics of Country/Rustic styles. (See "American Country (or Rustic) Styles" pages 144–150)

5. Identify characteristics of Neoclassic styles. (See "Neoclassic" pages 150–157)

Historic Style Influences: Late Nineteenth Century and Beyond

From the end of the nineteenth and into the twentieth century, aesthetic design became a consideration in the design of kitchens and bathrooms along with function. This was due to several factors: The continued movement of plumbing indoors, eventually a code requirement; an increase in urban living as jobs moved from farms to cities; and the increased effect of the Industrial Revolution with the creation of new materials, products, technologies, and mass production. Single-family home building in the United States was expanding, along with the means to disseminate plans and other information about them to consumers, creating a demand and a culture of consumption. There was an increased interest in design as architecture and "decorating" academic programs and shelter publications expanded, exposing average citizens to new ideas and technologies, fueling a demand for them. An unintentional but real effect was that of Hollywood and the motion picture industry. As that industry grew in the 1920s and 1930s, sets were created with elaborate bathrooms and bedrooms as backdrops. After World War II, more technological developments, a result of the war effort, could be applied to the home, building was booming along with the population, and the availability of television helped to advertise and spread these design ideas, creating markets and demand. Kitchens were often settings for family-oriented television shows of the 1950s, 1960s, and 1970s, showing the latest styles, colors and developments. Many of these actual home interiors, including kitchens and baths, remain today, although not always as originally built. Clients who own these homes often want to preserve or return them to the character of the original interior style. Thus, designers need to understand these architectural and interior styles to assist clients with preservation.

Learning Objective 1: Identify and apply the steps for creating a historic theme from the late nineteenth and twentieth centuries for a kitchen or bathroom project.

Learning Objective 2: Identify significant historic architectural and interior design styles and details from the late nineteenth and twentieth centuries used in residential design.

Learning Objective 3: Apply characteristics of a selected historic style from this period to the design of kitchens and bathrooms.

ARTS AND CRAFTS

Not everyone favored changes created by technology and the industrialization of the nine-teenth century. Several artisan and religious movements fought against the culture and life-style of Victorian England and America and the resulting widening gap between the working class and the well-to-do business owners. The Industrial Revolution caused families to leave rural settings and move to the cities for work, where living accommodations were difficult and harsh. Decorative articles mass-produced for the emerging working class were shoddy and poorly made. There are scholars who believe the nineteenth century and Victorian design in particular to be a low point in western taste and design.

The Arts and Crafts movement of the late nineteenth and early twentieth centuries began around the mid-nineteenth century by craftsmen in England and North America who were incensed by the poor quality and design of early machine-made furnishings. The movement began in England, through the work of John Ruskin and William Morris, and quickly moved across the ocean to the United States.

The Arts and Crafts followers believed that with renewed appreciation for finely handcrafted objects, a return to rural, even medieval values was possible. The simplicity and craftsmanship of the Shaker style and preindustrial Japanese art were prized and collected. The Swedish country style has many parallels to the Arts and Crafts movement as well. The underlying emphasis was on simplicity of line, simple geometric ornamentation, and quality handcrafted elegance.

The Arts and Crafts design philosophy, to reestablish individual quality in design and objects was the foundation for Gustav Stickley's Arts and Crafts interiors and furniture designs. Also emerging out of the Arts and Crafts styling yet retaining its basic tenets was the Prairie School of Design founded by a group of Chicago area artists and architects who based their ideas and principles on the early 1889 to 1910 work of Frank Lloyd Wright. Wright's home designs were integrated into the surrounding predominantly prairie landscape, creating some of the most famous residences in North America, lasting well into the 1920s and 1930s. His strong midwestern roots led him to design prairie homes appropriate for cold winters and hot sum-mers with low roofs, long overhangs, and intricate, handmade, leaded-glass windows used in place of draperies. In contrast, California-style bungalow homes were relatively small (an exception is the architecture of the Gamble House in Pasadena, California, designed by the architects Greene and Greene). In the United States these styles arose at a time of a tremen-dous amount of home construction in widely expanding urban areas across the country. Many of these houses were sold in the form of kits, ordered through catalogs, including Sears and Roebuck, and erected onsite throughout the United States. These houses demonstrated an appreciation for the millwork and architectural detailing of the midwestern master design-ers. The modestly scaled and affordably priced homes had simplified molding details along with abundant built-in cabinetry. Many of these homes still exist today.

Arts and Crafts–Inspired Kitchens and Bathrooms

By the 1920s and 1930s, kitchens and bathrooms had for the most part moved indoors as a part of the main house structure, although they were separate and distinct rooms. First they continued to be primarily work/functional spaces rather than being focused on the design or aesthetics. These rooms were generally at the back of the house; the kitchen was strictly a workspace, where guests generally did not go. Bathrooms (often the size of a closet) were part of the private space, usually adjacent to bedrooms or the kitchen for plumbing considerations. Along with plumbing moving indoors, electricity became more commonplace, expanding the design options, including appliances and lighting. However, during the more prosperous 1920s, between the rise in popu-larity of home shelter magazines and the growing film industry, wealthy individuals were able to afford and have larger, more elaborately and well-crafted work and private spaces, many of which have remained intact, or been re-created, or adapted. The Arts and Crafts–inspired up-to-date kitchen in Figure 6.1 illustrates the use of the built-in simple oak cabinets, plain hard-ware, and authentic tiles reminiscent of that era along with the use of Frank Lloyd Wright–inspired pendant and wall sconce light fixtures. An Arts and Crafts–inspired bathroom, with the simple, dark-stained cabinetry and extensive use of slate tile is seen in Figure 6.2.

FIGURE 6.1 Arts and Crafts–inspired kitchen
Design by Brigette C. Fabi, CMKBD, Drury Design Kitchen & Bath Studio, Glen Ellyn, IL
Photo by Eric Hausman

Arts and Crafts–inspired design elements:

Cabinetry/millwork. Plain, solid-wood cabinetry and furniture arranged in a functional manner is popular. Typically it is abundant throughout the house, large in scale, simple in design, and primarily constructed of oak, although originally many California homes used the easily available redwood. Care was taken to showcase the grain of the wood, the methods of joinery, and hardware. Arts and Crafts designs today often use hickory, ash, cherry, or other similarly colored or stained fruitwood in place of oak.

Hardware/fixtures. Almost any brushed (and not shiny) finish or metal is used, especially copper, pewter, and wrought iron. Intricately patterned or hammered metalwork provides an authentic accent for fixtures.

Countertops. Natural or synthetic products that emphasize the inherent natural qualities of the real material (i.e., the strength of natural stone, especially slate; the depth of highly glazed, multicolored porcelain pottery; and the matte finish of rough earthenware-type materials, especially handmade ceramic tile) are popular.

Floors. Plain or simple geometric patterns in slate, tile, or wood are most common. Also used were Native American patterns or other handcrafted materials. True linoleum or vinyl in patterns of the period with matte finishes are also common.

FIGURE 6.2 Arts and Crafts–inspired bathroom
Design by Jacqueline Balint, CKD, The Kitchen Collection LLC, Redondo Beach, CA
Larry A. Falke Photography

Walls. Typical wall coverings are tooled leather, wood paneling, paint in solid colors, and wallpapers that are block printed with subtle, stylized floral or animal patterns (like those of William Morris) or strong geometrics with repeats.

Ceilings and lighting. A popular ceiling treatment is textured plaster with natural wood beams. Decorative light fixtures with stained glass shades from the Tiffany era or simple amber glass are used. Mission-style wall and ceiling light fixtures, crafted in copper or pewter, or decorative Art Nouveau or Japanese fixtures are also found.

Colors. A wide range of muted (grayed) colors is popular, such as golden yellow, soft greens, blue-greens, and blues drawn from nature. Colors are based on and derived from natural dyes, earth tones, and indigo blue.

Representative motifs. Popular are stylized plant and animal motifs, especially those of William Morris, strong geometric patterns, and Native American motifs.

Fabrics. Natural fibers such as cottons, linens, and nubby wools are woven into a variety of fabrics, including tapestries and velvet. Printed cotton and linen fabrics in particular and leather are also popular.

Accents/accessories. Arts and Crafts and Mission-style furniture and accessories, Shaker and Native American objects, brushed and hammered copper and pewter, Japanese ceramic and metal craft pieces, and handmade and glazed ceramic tile in typical patterns of the period all are popular.

Associated styles. Renaissance, Gothic, Shaker, Spanish Mission, Art Nouveau, Japanese.

ART NOUVEAU

The Art Nouveau design period extended from the late nineteenth century (1890) to the beginning of World War I (1914). It followed the changes brought about during the Industrial Revolution throughout Europe and the United States throughout the nineteenth century. In Paris, young artists sought to utilize newfound technological inventions and materials to create objects based on natural elements rather than using historical precedents. Much of the work of these young artists was showcased at the Paris Exhibition of 1889. Out of this came the Art Nouveau design movement, seen primarily on the continent of Europe in France, Spain, and Belgium. This movement influenced others as well, the Scotsman Charles Rennie Mackintosh and Americans Louis Sullivan of Chicago and Louis Comfort Tiffany of New York. The De Stijl movement of Gerrit Rietveld in Holland and the Wiener Werkstätte of Josef Hoffman in Austria also emerged from Art Nouveau.

Art Nouveau–Inspired Kitchens and Bathrooms

Art Nouveau was a relatively short-lived design movement, a reaction to the mass production of industrialization, and ended rather abruptly with the onset of World War I in Europe. The Art Nouveau design influences were an impetus for the Art Deco design movement, which developed after the war. Examples of Art Nouveau architecture and design remain today, particularly in Europe. Occasionally one sees an Art Nouveau–inspired kitchen, although Art Nouveau serves as the inspiration for a bathroom somewhat more frequently. Cabinetry, wall treatments, fixture design, and accessories are common uses of Art Nouveau designs as seen in the kitchen and bath in Figures 6.3 and 6.4.

Art Nouveau–inspired design elements:

Cabinetry/millwork. A variety of woods are popular (from light to dark, also painted), including oak, walnut, mahogany, ash, and fruitwoods, with emphasis on the grain, elaborate carving, usually with curvilinear forms, natural motifs, and moldings.

Hardware/fixtures. Brass and almost any other metals, usually brushed finish, are popular, in curvilinear shapes and designs.

Countertops. Natural materials or those that simulate them are popular for countertops.

Floors. Popular are wood floors in parquet patterns, elaborate inlays of contrasting wood in curvilinear patterns, ceramic or stone tiles, and hand-woven area rugs and carpets.

Walls. Typical wall coverings are paint, in a soft solid color, elaborately carved plaster or wood paneling, or wallpapers in natural, curvilinear patterns.

Ceilings and lighting. Textured plaster with natural wood beams and curved moldings with natural carving are popular for ceilings. Tiffany and Tiffany-inspired glass and stained glass are popular for lighting fixtures.

Colors. A wide range of colors are used, from soft muted pastels to dark turquoise. Lavender and purple are especially popular, along with black and white.

Representative motifs. Popular are asymmetrical flowing, nature-inspired curves, often with whiplike or undulating curved ends, patterns inspired by a variety of cultures (i.e., Vikings, Middle Eastern), floral fantasies, and other plantlike and animal motifs, including dragonflies and other insects.

Fabrics. Velvets, satins, or printed fabrics made of natural fibers, such as cottons, linens, and silks, are common.

FIGURE 6.3 Art Nouveau–inspired kitchen

Design by Artur Leyzerov, codesigner Oleg Vasyliychuk, Symphony Kitchens Inc., Mississauga, ON
Roy Timm Photography

Accents/accessories. Common are Art Nouveau–inspired glass, ceramics, metalwork, Japanese art prints, Aubrey Beardsley prints, and Arts and Crafts–inspired fabrics.

Associated styles. French Rococo, Art Deco, Japanese, some Arts and Crafts.

ART DECO

After World War I (1918), a theme for interior design known as Art Moderne or Art Deco was introduced in France, inspired by and named for the 1925 Exposition Internationale des Arts Décoratifs et Industriels Modernes in Paris. This style, which was popular during the between-war period of the 1920s,1930s, and early 1940s, is considered an outgrowth of the Art Nouveau design movement, which ended abruptly with the onset of World War I. Art Deco was first used primarily with furnishings then spread to interior and exterior architecture after the discovery of King Tut's tomb in 1922. This led to an Egyptian motif focus within the design world. The emerging technology and use of newly developed man-made materials, such as plastics, expanded design options and opportunities for designers. Art Deco gained momentum as architects and designers stripped away the ornamentation of the Victorian era and introduced to the Western world designs from other forgotten and diverse cultures, such as the Vikings and Mayans, other art forms like the Russian ballet, and to maximize the power and use of industrial invention for design. Improved communication and transportation allowed for the spread of design ideas around the world more quickly than before this time. The growing large cities in the United States embraced this style during the prosperous 1920s, creating skyscrapers including the Chrysler and Empire State buildings in New York City, both completed in the early 1930s, then again with the

FIGURE 6.4 Art Nouveau–inspired bathroom
Design by Elina Katsioula-Beall, CKD, Dewitt Designer Kitchens, Pasadena, CA
Photo by Suki Medencevic

post-Depression-era government building projects that flourished during the 1930s. Hollywood, the young motion picture industry, and consumer accessibility to shelter publications featuring design allowed these new ideas and products to be widely viewed, further inspiring designers and clients and creating a demand for them to be mass-produced. Much of Art Deco design style and influence endures to the present day throughout Europe and the United States.

Art Deco–Inspired Kitchens and Bathrooms

The design ideas of the multifaceted Art Deco design movement found their way into kitchens and bathrooms during this between world war time period as building of single-family homes flourished across the United States. In kitchens and bathrooms, the colors of the period in particular, especially the contrast of light with black, were found in the materials for floors, walls, and countertops and eventually in fixtures. The typical designs were most often found in tile work, on floors, countertops, and on walls. The Art Deco contrast of black and white and both straight and curved lines are illustrated in the kitchen in Figure 6.5. The bathroom in Figure 6.6 shows an Art Deco style tile design, pedestal sink, typically curved wall sconces and mirror as well as the color contrast of black and yellow

FIGURE 6.5 Art Deco–inspired black and white kitchen
Design by Friedemann Weinhardt, Design First Kitchen Interiors, Ottawa, ON
Photo by Marc Fowler, Metropolis Studio

Art Deco–inspired design elements:

Cabinetry/millwork. A variety of woods are used, stained or painted to the desired color and finish, from light to dark, matte to shiny. Steel or other metal cabinets, often painted, were introduced at the time.

Hardware/fixtures. Metals, brass, steel, pewter, both shiny and matte finishes are common.

Countertops. Natural materials or those that simulate them, and ceramic tile are used.

Floors. Linoleum, ceramic tile, wood, or stone are also used for floors. Hexagonal or diagonal shapes and patterns are common.

Walls. Typical wallcoverings are paint in a solid color ceramic tile, or wallpapers in a variety of printed patterns using typical period motifs or elaborate graphics or scenic designs. Glass block is used in both kitchens and bathrooms, adding light to the space.

Ceilings and lighting. Plain ceilings, either white or matching the wall color, are used. For lighting, glass fixtures with metal trim in a variety of typical shapes and motifs are used.

Colors. A wide range of colors are used, from soft muted pastels to dark, yellow, lavender, turquoise, with black and white contrasts are popular choices.

FIGURE 6.6 Art Deco–influenced bathroom
Design by Linda McKenna, CKD, CBD, Custom Kitchens by John Wilkins, Inc, Oakland, CA
Yvonne D. Williams Photography

Representative motifs. A variety of motifs and geometric shapes, including the triangle, zigzag, thunderbolt, horizontal lines, Aztec and Mayan pyramids, skyscrapers, waterfall, and scallop are common.

Fabrics. Natural fibers are used, such as cottons, linens, silks in velvet or satin fabrics. Rayon and acetate fabrics began to be used.

Accents/accessories. Art Deco–inspired glass, ceramics, metalwork are popular, as are objects from a variety of cultures around the world from what were considered little known and exotic places, such as South America, Africa, the Far East, and the Middle East.

Associated styles: Art Nouveau, Japanese, some Arts and Crafts, Bauhaus, Scandinavian, midcentury modern, postmodern.

BAUHAUS (INTERNATIONAL MODERN)

Because this style was a significant departure from traditional construction methods and materials, the Eiffel Tower is often considered the first building of the International School of Architecture. The tower was commissioned in 1887 to commemorate the Exposition Universelle (1889), the Paris Exposition of 1889. However, in fact, the style known as International Modern began at the Bauhaus School of Design in Weimar (then in Dessau), Germany, which operated from 1919 until 1933 and created the first steel and glass structures using technology and materials it developed. With restrictions and controls placed on architects and designers in the 1930s by the Nazi regime in Germany, many of the founding European architects and designers, including Walter Gropius, Ludwig Mies van der Rohe, and Marcel Breuer, closed the Bauhaus school and moved to the United States. They led and taught at several renowned architectural schools and universities, bringing the ideas of the Bauhaus to the curriculum of these architecture and design programs. The International School of Architecture created by these masters influenced and dominated design through the 1970s.

Bauhaus–Inspired Kitchens and Bathrooms

The Bauhaus with its international influence and ideas was incorporated into the interior architectural design of homes with the sleek industrial look and use of metal (primarily steel), natural materials such as stone, and newly created materials (plastic and laminates). The influence was seen primarily in the kitchen, as technological developments in appliances and fixtures had advanced, creating new and multiple options. Standards for cabinetry design and kitchen planning were developed. The Bauhaus style influenced bathrooms to a lesser degree, primarily simplifying cabinetry and expanding fixture design. The kitchen seen in Figure 6.7 and the bathroom seen in Figure 6.8 are examples of the Bauhaus influence in the design of these spaces in contemporary homes.

Bauhaus–inspired design elements:

Cabinetry/millwork. Common are industrial materials including steel and other metals for cabinets, some use of laminates, wood veneers, with simple lines and geometric shapes.

Hardware/fixtures. Metals, simple, smooth, and straight shapes, shiny and matte finishes are used.

Countertops. Natural materials such as stone (or simulated stone), plastic laminates, and plain ceramic tile are used for countertops.

Floors. Linoleum or tile is common; stone and wood are also used.

Walls. Plain paint in white or other solid color is used.

Ceilings and lighting. Plain, often white ceilings are common. Lighting fixtures with simple straight lines, of unadorned gray-colored metal and translucent white glass are common.

Colors. Neutral colors predominate—black, gray, and white—often with a single color accent, commonly a primary color.

FIGURE 6.7 Bauhaus–inspired kitchen
Design by Kimberly Larzelere, Kimberly Larzelere Interiors, Redwood City, CA
Photo by David Duncan Livingston

Representative motifs. Rectangular and geometric lines and shapes, are popular, if used at all. The form of the object is the motif; little, if any, applied pattern or decoration is used.

Fabrics. Common are natural fibers, such as cottons, linens, wools, and leather, generally solid rather than patterned, although some abstract or stylized "natural" animal-hide patterns are used as accents.

Accents/accessories. Bauhaus-inspired glass, ceramics, metalwork, furniture, fabrics, and simple objects are popular.

Associated styles. Art Deco, Arts and Crafts (especially the work of Frank Lloyd Wright), Scandinavian modern, midcentury modern, postmodern, Italian and European modern.

SCANDINAVIAN MODERN

After World War I (during the 1920s and 1930s) in the north of Europe, technology from the continent, primarily from the Bauhaus, was incorporated into architectural and furniture designs as the Scandinavian countries recovered from the war. Designers used wood and

FIGURE 6.8 Bauhaus–inspired bathroom

Design by Christine Pandur, AKBD and Tammy MacKay, AKBD, Design Eye Ltd., Edmonton, AB

other natural materials, which were plentiful in those areas. These predominantly simple, uncluttered designs also became popular in the United States after World War II, as several Scandinavian designers and architects fled their countries for the United States prior to and after the war (most notably Alvar Aalto and father and son Eliel and Eero Saarinen). Other significant Scandinavian designers were Finn Juhl, Hans Wegner, Jens Risom, and Arne Jacobsen, whose furniture was popular from World War II through the 1960s. Scandinavian modern designs became popular in the 1920s and 1930s and continued after World War II. This Scandinavian design influence was apparent in the 1950s style known as Danish modern, and continues in the designs of IKEA® furnishings and cabinetry.

Scandinavian Modern–Inspired Kitchens and Bathrooms

The use of wood and stone, rather than steel or other manufactured materials, characterizes Scandinavian Modern kitchens and bathrooms, along with the simple uncluttered lines of the Bauhaus. The natural look of simple, light or medium toned solid wood or wood veneer faced cabinetry became popular for both kitchens and bathrooms (see Figures 6.9 and 6.10). The furniture, especially stools and chairs, of a noted Scandinavian designer is often found as seating.

FIGURE 6.9 Scandinavian modern–inspired kitchen
Courtesy of Wood-Mode Fine Custom Cabinetry, Inc.

Scandinavian modern–inspired design elements

Cabinetry/millwork. Wood is the primary material for cabinetry and millwork, often a laminated wood veneer faced plywood, rather than solid wood. Light-colored native hardwoods, such as birch and beech, are popular; teak is also used.

Hardware/fixtures. Wood knobs and metals (typically brushed and silver in color), simple, straight shapes, matte finishes are common.

Countertops. Popular are natural materials or those that simulate them (laminates primarily), with either a solid color, stone, or a wood-grain look.

Floors. Linoleum or wood is common; stone and simple or natural-looking tile also are used.

Walls. Wood paneling, stone, or paint in a solid color is popular, with large window expanses.

Ceilings and lighting. Solid colors, usually white or other light color, predominate. Simple, Bauhaus style fixtures in metal and translucent glass are common for light fixtures.

Colors. Neutrals predominate: light natural tones of beige or white with a single color accent, commonly blue, red, or black.

FIGURE 6.10 Scandinavian modern–inspired bathroom
Design by Victoria Shaw, Binns Kitchen + Bath Design, Pickering, ON
Photo by Tim McClean Photography

Representative motifs. Popular are stylized natural, generally plant images, rectangular and geometric motifs, stripes, and diamonds. The form and material of the object is the motif, and little, if any, applied decoration is used.

Fabrics: Natural fibers, such as cottons, linens, wools, and leather, are used. Generally they are solid or textured rather than patterned, although some stylized and abstract patterns are used as accents.

Accents/accessories: Scandinavian-inspired glass, ceramics, metalwork, fabrics, rugs (rya rugs), and simple objects are popular.

Associated styles. Art Deco, Arts and Crafts (especially the work of Frank Lloyd Wright), Bauhaus, Shaker, midcentury modern, postmodern, Italian and European Modern.

MIDCENTURY MODERN

Sometimes referred to as retro, which is slang for "retrospective," midcentury modern styling emerges with optimism, exuberance, and self-confidence—exhibited in bold colors and patterns—within the American design community at the end of World War II. This style was popular from the late 1940s, through the 1950s, 1960s, and into the 1970s. At the time, changes in design and technology were occurring and at a rapid rate. With soldiers returning to the United States after World War II and the baby boom population increase came new demands for housing, furnishings, and other consumer goods. The new technology that was developed and used for the war effort then shifted to consumer goods, including fixtures, appliances, and manufactured synthetic materials and fabrics. In addition to new materials, designers were working with shape and form in different ways, sculpting them into simple curved shapes. Some designers found working in glass, concrete, and steel structures to be cold and dehumanizing; thus, wood became a popular home-building material again. The single-story ranch style house design of California architect Cliff May became widespread throughout the United States. Joseph Eichler and the Eichler style homes with their central atrium and wide expanses of glass also became popular. In the 1950s and 1960s, industrial designers experimented with bright, bold colors and new materials for interior applications, including for furniture, appliances, cabinetry, and fixtures. Noted among these are Ray and Charles Eames, Eero Saarinen, and George Nelson. Their designs made both the home and the work space more functional and visually interesting, reflecting the prosperity of the postwar period and creating the style known as midcentury modernism or retro. The demand for consumer goods was high, and technology kept improving on them at a rapid pace. Television and advertising was wide-spread and assisted with this creation of demand. With planned obsolescence (obsolescence was built in), consumers would want the latest goods and replace them frequently with the newest versions.

Midcentury Modern Kitchens and Bathrooms

This midcentury modern design look was seen in the kitchens and bathrooms of these postwar homes. Family life changed and house plans opened up, giving the illusion of a larger space. The kitchen was integrated into dining and social spaces, especially the fast-becoming-popular family room. The kitchen no longer was just a functional workspace, separate from the rest of the rooms in the house, but an integral part of the entire interior. Thus, it became important for color and style to coordinate with the rest of interior and have well designed and the latest fixtures and appliances. Technology helped to provide this. As one peruses the advertisements for products of this period, it is not unusual to see the "typical" American family shown, the wife/mother cooking or washing dishes, with one of their children (the father and/or husband notably absent from the kitchen at this time) (see Figure 6.11).

The bathroom also saw changes, particularly with style and updated fixtures, an increase in the room size to accommodate a growing family, and the greater use of color for fixtures and other finish materials, much as with the kitchen. (Refer to the applicable bathroom images in Chapter 1, "Brief History of Kitchen and Bathroom Design.")

There are two major versions of midcentury modernism. First is a design discipline celebrating the post-war prosperity, brightly colored new materials, and products that grew out of the world of chemistry. Designers used new, lightweight materials, such as fiberglass, cast aluminum, laminates, acrylic, and resin, to create interesting furniture pieces and abstract accessories. Intense, clear colors were used everywhere in this version of midcentury modernism, reflecting this optimism (see Figure 6.12). The second midcentury styling is linked to designs originating in Scandinavia prior to and just after World War II. American designers Charles and Ray Eames, along with Scandinavians Alvar Aalto and Hans Wegner, led the way with a focus on natural woods, such as teak and veneered plywood, combined with much softer, subtle colors, such as faded chartreuse green, and turquoise, with white accents (see Figure 6.13).

Since the end of the twentieth century, re-creating or restoring a midcentury modern kitchen and or bathroom has become popular, as clients seek out the well-built ranch style and Eichler homes of that time period. The kitchen and bath designer must understand the design elements of the two versions of midcentury modern style to successfully assist clients with these kitchen and bathroom designs.

Midcentury modern–inspired design elements:

   Cabinetry/millwork. Teak and mahogany, as well as almost any straight-grained wood veneer for cabinets and doors are common. Painted metal, brushed stainless steel, chrome,

Kohler Sinks for modern kitchens

The Clearfield in Sunrise

Picture the pleasure of using this Kohler sink in Sunrise color, cheerful as a song, that brightens a whole kitchen. Measure your tasks to its spacious convenience—you'll almost feel them lighten—with the two roomy basins, ample sanitary drainboards, features everywhere that foretell ease and pride.

There are Kohler sinks for every space and preference, in six colors and white. The enamel—reliably acid-resisting, easy to clean—is fused to a base of iron cast in one piece for rigidity. The chrome-plated fittings are all brass for maximum resistance to wear and corrosion.

Consult your Kohler dealer. Write for booklet 3-C.

KOHLER CO. *Established 1873* KOHLER, WIS.

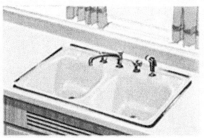

The Delafield in Peachblow

KOHLER of KOHLER

ENAMELED IRON AND VITREOUS CHINA PLUMBING FIXTURES • BRASS FITTINGS • ELECTRIC PLANTS • AIR-COOLED ENGINES • PRECISION CONTROLS

FIGURE 6.11 1950s Kohler advertisement featuring color in kitchen fixtures
Courtesy of Kohler Company

FIGURE 6.12 Midcentury modern–inspired kitchen

Design by Elina Katsioula-Beall, CKD, Dewitt Designer Kitchens, Pasadena, CA
Photo by Suki Medencevic

and nickel are also used. Frosted glass, ribbon glass, or wire-reinforced commercial glass is used for cabinetry door inserts. Cabinets can also be accented with aluminum or brightly colored (usually plastic laminate) accent doors.

Hardware/fixtures. Asymmetrically balanced, interesting but simply shaped or straight lined, half-round or knob hardware that is understated, usually brushed metal hardware is appropriate.

Countertops. Laminate (gold speckled, marble look, or boomerang patterns are typical), stainless steel, engineered stone, and quartz surfaces in bright colors are appropriate. Decorative tiles are used at the backsplash in white or bright colors. Red is popular, but others are also used to contrast with white.

Floors. Cork and linoleum flooring are the most common, as is vinyl (sheets or tiles) that simulates natural patterns. Strip wood flooring is used occasionally. If tile is used, small, narrow grout lines and sharp tile edges are preferable over more irregular edges.

Walls. Typically walls are painted plain colors or papered with fruit, florals, or popular kitchen- or bath-themed patterns. As an accent on kitchen walls, either neutral or colors, are 3- by 6-inch brick installed in a running bond pattern (subway style) as well as the use of glass block.

Ceilings and lighting. Simple white painted ceilings are normally used. Shiny or brushed chrome metal fixtures with milky glass diffusers in simple geometric shapes are typical for lighting fixtures

FIGURE 6.13 Midcentury modern–inspired bathroom
Design by Jon Crabtree, Inspired Spaces, Minneapolis, MN
Photo by sphotodesign

Colors. In the colorful version of this design theme, black-and-white repetitive patterns with pale tones of yellow and blue, peach or mid-greens, and blue greens are one choice. Pop art in acid green, orange, pink, red, yellow, and/or bright blue is another colorway that is appropriate. Brown and orange or avocado green and harvest gold is a third possible color way. In a simpler design version, maple red, chartreuse green, chestnut orange, black, pearl gray, and coral red are possible colors. Of note, mixing black or white in either version works. Woods are natural in finish so they blend.

Representative motifs. Popular motifs are florals, fruit, kitchen- and bath-thematic patterns, strong geometrics, and pop art.

Fabrics. Cotton prints in bright colors are used primarily, including patterns of designers such as Vera, Alexander Girard, Charles and Ray Eames, Marimekko, Verner Panton, and Jack Lenor Larsen.

Accents/accessories. Antique and reproduction period kitchenware is appropriate, such as Fiestaware; Harlequin dinnerware; Bakelite-handled cutlery; molded plastics including Melmac; and Russel Wright ceramic dinnerware. Reproduction 1950s and 1960s furniture, such as that of Charles and Ray Eames, Eero Saarinen, George Nelson, and Harry Bertoia, in chrome and laminate, or Scandinavian wood pieces are also appropriate in these spaces. Michael Graves inspired kitchen accessories and reproduction major and portable appliances are also appropriate for the midcentury modern look.

Associated styles. Art Deco, Arts and Crafts (the work of Frank Lloyd Wright), Bauhaus, Scandinavian modern, Shaker, Italian and European modern, postmodern.

ITALIAN AND EUROPEAN MODERN POSTWAR INFLUENCES, URBAN CONTEMPORARY

With the rebuilding of Europe after the devastation of World War II, beginning in the late 1940s and into the 1950s, opportunities for new and innovative designs developed, as housing and consumer goods of all kinds were needed. This was due in part to the influx of money from the United States and allies to assist with this rebuilding. Some in the architecture and design fields feel that Italy used this opportunity and took design and innovation for interior spaces and goods to new heights, surpassing France—Paris in particular—which had been considered by most to be where new designs and styles first appeared since the time of Louis XIV in the seventeenth century. New innovations in modern design and technology were introduced in the industrial city of Milan in the north of Italy, continuing today at the annual Milan Furniture Fair held each spring. Sleek, uncluttered, functional designs and spaces, often industrial in nature, with the latest technology and design materials are the norm.

This style has a sophisticated preference for minimalism in materials, decoration, and interior design elements. Since the 1980s, this Italian modern or Euro-look or high-tech look is often called urban or contemporary modernism, even minimalism. Probably best executed by Italian and other European industrial and furniture designers, it focuses on simplicity and functionality yet provides great textural and visual interest in the materials selected.

Italian/European Modern Kitchens and Bathrooms

Since the 1980s, this Italian/European modern style, popular in kitchens and bathrooms, typically has been described as an emphasis on simple architectural shapes, with strong lineal interest created by blocks of space defined by the connected cabinetry and wall elements. Unadorned, structural, often industrial materials are featured as a backdrop (think of a big-city loft with its oversize windows and brick walls, or an entire wall of glass in a typical single-family residence). Today's Italian/European modern design for kitchens and bathrooms continues to be based on sleek, simple architectural designs (see Figures 6.14 and 6.15).

FIGURE 6.14 Italian/European modern kitchen
Design by Claire Reimann, AKBD, Jason Good Custom Cabinets, Victoria, BC
Photo by Joshua Lawrence

Italian/European modern–inspired design elements:

Cabinetry/millwork. Oak, teak, birch, maple, or other popular woods are appropriate. Straight, simple grains prevail. In many of these rooms, the cabinetry doors are not wood but stainless steel, acrylic/polyester in gloss or matte finishes, laminates, or painted surfaces. Although most of the doors are slab doors, narrowly dimensioned stile-and-rail doors are also appropriate. Aluminum frame doors that feature frosted, ribbed, or other geometrically patterned glass accent many designs.

Hardware/fixtures. Typically chrome, stainless steel, or nickel is used. Polished metal including brass are appropriate, in simple, straight shapes.

Countertops. Stainless steel, concrete, and natural stone are appropriate choices along with manufactured surfaces that simulate them.

Floors. There are several options: a worn wide-plank pine floor or a unique exotic dark wood such as wenge, or almost a bleached, narrow-plank light maple. Vinyl or engineered flooring that simulate natural materials is a possibility, as is concrete (gray or painted a color) or cork flooring.

Walls. Typically walls, if they aren't all windows, are left unfinished as the building material or painted solid colors. Brick or concrete block is an appropriate material installed in a running bond pattern.

Ceilings and lighting. Simple painted ceilings are enhanced by open wood beams, skylights, or other architectural materials and elements, even existing mechanical equipment,

FIGURE 6.15 Italian/European modern bathroom
Design by Leslie Lamarre, CKD, CID, codesigners Erika Shjeflo and Casey Darcy, TRG Architects, Burlingame, CA
Bernard Andre Photography

within the room. Industrial lighting fixtures in a variety of metals and glass in simple shapes as well as track lighting are used.

Colors. A limiting factor for color is the client and designer's imagination. European designers often use large blocks of cabinetry in vibrant primary colors: blue, orange, red, lime green, or wood tones. Neutral colors including blacks and whites, blue-based grays, or yellow "taupe" grays are extremely popular. Stainless steel or other gray metal is a key accent material. An emerging popular color is a dark black-brown stain used on open-grained woods, such as oak or ash.

Representative motifs. Strong geometric patterns, rough and smooth textures, straight lines, and pop and abstract art motifs are popular.

Fabrics: Popular are cotton, linens, wools, leather, as well as synthetics that mimic these natural fibers. Fabrics by designers such as Alexander Girard, Charles and Ray Eames, Marimekko, Verner Panton, and Jack Lenor Larsen are used.

Accents/accessories. The resurgence of interest in retro furniture and accessories from midcentury industrial designers is appropriate; consider accents by Charles and Ray Eames, Eero Saarinen, and Harry Bertoia. The post-modern furniture of Michael Graves or Philippe Starck is also a choice. Combining commercial-type cooking equipment and storage racks (open stainless steel or copper racks) work well—as do open shelving and functional carts. Curvilinear, soft naturalistic wood furniture from Scandinavian designers, such as Alvar Aalto and Hans Wegner, in chairs and tables also work well.

Associated styles. Art deco, Arts and Crafts, Bauhaus, Scandinavian modern, Shaker and other country styles, midcentury modern, postmodern.

POSTMODERN

The architectural community began experimenting in new ways with historical motifs and design inspirations from the late 1970s into the 1980s. Michael Graves, an architect known today for his industrial design work in ergonomically correct yet architecturally elegant house wares and fixtures, is recognized as one of the founders of Postmodern design. This type of design called on reinterpreting many of the geometric and traditional shapes of prior design styles, such as the Classical and Art Deco periods, and returning to a more vibrant use of color. The basis of Postmodern design, which influences the spaces of today, is its focus on complexity, not stark simplification. The style synthesizes design history and symbolic content rather than relying on purely functional reductionism.

Postmodern-Inspired Kitchens and Bathrooms

Postmodern kitchens and bathrooms are simple in design with hints of the classical, if not a playful influence and interpretation. Michael Graves and his designs of faucets and other kitchen and bath fixtures for Delta and those for kitchen utensils and portable appliances, first for Target and currently JC Penney, are examples. While using primarily classical elements in simplified form (lacking some of the traditional ornamentation), one characteristic and recurring design element is the round, circular form of the oculus, usually in the form or a window or molding or other features in the space or on the object (see Figures 6.16 and 6.17). Other design elements in both kitchens and bathrooms are simplified classical ones, usually with curves, and sometimes hardly discernible. Any patterns used have classical design inspiration, usually a stylized version, and are kept to a minimum.

Postmodern-inspired design elements:

Cabinetry/millwork. Oak, teak, birch, maple, or other popular woods are appropriate. Straight grains in veneers prevail. In many of these rooms, the cabinetry doors are not wood but laminates or painted surfaces. Although most doors are slab doors, narrowly dimensioned European stile-and-rail doors are used as well. These doors could feature frosted, ribbed, or other patterned glass accents in simple designs.

FIGURE 6.16 Postmodern-inspired kitchen
Design by Tim Scott, codesigner Erica Westeroth, CKD, XTC Design Inc., Toronto, ON
Photo by Donna Griffith Photography

Hardware/fixtures. Typically chrome, stainless steel, or nickel is used. It usually is brushed rather than polished in simple straight shapes.

Countertops. Stainless steel, concrete, and natural stone are typical choices as well as laminates or engineered stones that have the look of natural products.

Floors. There are several options: One is a wide-plank wood floor (almost any wood) from dark to light. Vinyl, ceramic tile, or engineered wood floorings that simulate natural materials are a possibility, as is natural stone, concrete, or cork flooring.

Walls. Painted plain wall colors are used, as are stone and wood or materials that simulate these products.

Ceilings and lighting. Open wood or painted beams, skylights, or other architectural materials and elements within the room enhance simple painted ceilings. Recessed cans, track or simple pendant light fixtures are typical lighting fixtures.

Colors. Neutral colors in blacks, whites, beiges, blue-based gray or taupe grays, and browns are extremely popular.

Representative motifs. Strong geometric patterns, straight lines, the oculus, stylized classically inspired motifs, pop and abstract art are common.

FIGURE 6.17 Postmodern-inspired bathroom

Design by Sheena Hammond, codesigners Erica Westeroth, CKD, NCIDQ and Tim Scott, XTC Design Inc., Toronto, ON
Photo by Arnal Photography

Fabrics: Plain and textured cottons, linens, wools, leather, as well as synthetics that mimic these natural fibers, are used. Prints reminiscent of classical Greece and Rome as well as the Italian countryside are popular.

Accents/accessories. The Postmodern furniture of Michael Graves, Philippe Starck, Harry Bertoia, or Frank Gehry is a choice. The kitchen and household utensils, and portable appliances of Michael Graves, are popular.

Associated styles. Ancient Greek and Roman, Art Deco, Arts and Crafts, Bauhaus, Scandinavian modern, Shaker and other country styles, midcentury modern.

TWENTY-FIRST CENTURY AND BEYOND

End of the Twentieth Century: A Return to Roots

During the 1980s, then into the early twenty-first century, and especially after the terrorist attacks of September 11, 2001, many interior designers and clients returned to the safety, security, elegance, and warmth of selected European and American historical environments. Popular among designers and home builders were Spanish and Tuscan villas, reminiscent of the Italian and Spanish Renaissance; kitchens and bathrooms were designed to reflect the inside of these villas as well, yet with all the modern amenities. Old World artisan techniques were re-created on everything from wallpaper to tiles, and faux painting becoming a popular and highly valued skill.

Also part of this return to roots was the developing interest in re-creating in new construction or restoring to as near the original as possible older homes or styles, dating back as far as the seventeenth or eighteenth century, but with all the modern amenities and conveniences and complying with current building codes and functional requirements. These styles ranged from various colonial American styles; European styles of the English, French, Spanish, and Italian; various Victorian styles (each discussed in Chapter 5), the Arts and Crafts and Bungalow style; international modern (Bauhaus); and the variety of Art Deco steel and glass structures, to the single-story ranch and Eichler homes of the midcentury modern and beyond (covered in this chapter).

Throughout the 1990s and into the twenty-first century, an emerging interest in a softer version of contemporary styling developed. This style was based on the subtleties of Asian concepts of beauty, the calming effects of Asian/Pacific Rim design, along with the clean, uncluttered, almost industrial lines of the Italian/European styling. Chapter 7 presents selected examples of these styles along with other diverse cultural and eclectic design influences for kitchens and bathrooms.

The return to design elements and styles from past eras remains a popular trend in interior design.

Other Considerations

Detailed discussion of twentieth-century historical data is the way for the designer to begin building an understanding of these architectural styles and interior elements. Seeing and naming different elements of past artistry assists designers in differentiating between styles that can be quite similar.

When considering how to separate or to match styles with historic collections, remember that most design styles did not have specific start or stop dates. Rather they overlapped as emerging styles, frequently borrowing features from one that was declining in popularity while adding new characteristics moving forward to develop into a succeeding style. Usually a new style appeared at the top end of the market first while older designs continued to permeate slowly down to the middle and working classes. The top of the market was also the first to benefit from the latest technological developments and newest products and materials. Often individual features of a new style were tacked on to existing dwellings, creating transitional forms that bridged several styles. Additionally, the three social classes familiar to us today—upper, middle, and working—also continued to emerge, as the population became a predominantly urban one. Therefore, each style was available in various configurations appropriate for the more ornate upper-class dwellings; a more middle-class, moderate approach; and the simplest working person's version.

This talk of architectural history should not be overwhelming. The entire discussion is simply a starting point on which to build your unique design concept. Don't let it limit what and how you design by strictly defining "what goes with what." Just the opposite—understanding the details of past styles and the elements and principles of design should free designer, and clients, to create unique, new, and successful interpretations.

Rather than overcomplicate the definition of a certain theme, focus on the sense of the style. The combination of well-thought-out design details defined by a client's preferences is far more interesting—and satisfying—than a room created by slavishly following the rules established by historians.

SUMMARY

This chapter discusses architectural and interior design styles from the end of the nineteenth century, through the twentieth century, and into the beginning of the twenty-first century as they are applied to kitchens and bathrooms. These are the styles that designers will encounter most often when working with these spaces, building on the earlier styles discussed in Chapter 5. Because interior design has become more global in recent years, clients often seek to use a cultural, usually a non-Western, design influence in their spaces. Most typically these are from Asia, and selected influences are discussed in Chapter 7.

REVIEW QUESTIONS

1. Identify characteristics that differentiate Arts and Crafts style from Art Nouveau. (See "Arts and Crafts" pages 164–167 "Art Nouveau" pages 167–168)
2. Compare and contrast the significant design elements of the Bauhaus and Scandinavian Modern design styles. (See "Bauhaus (International Modern)" pages 172–173; "Scandinavian Modern" pages 173–176)
3. Identify significant characteristics of midcentury modern kitchens and bathrooms. (See "Midcentury Modern" pages 176–181)
4. What are some of the significant characteristics of the Italian/European modern style? (See "Italian/European Modern Kitchens and Bathrooms" pages 181–184)

Other Theme Design Influences and Eclectic Design

Most of the discussion of historical/theme designs has centered on the Western historical influences and styles that prevailed in Europe (and later the United States) for over 2,000 years. For about three-fourths of that time, most of these Europeans didn't travel far beyond their own borders; some never left the town or immediate area where they were born. Marco Polo and Christopher Columbus, among others, were some of the first to venture beyond what was considered known and familiar territory and then return to talk about it along with goods and ideas different from those in the West. Prior to their journeys, exposure to outside influences, including design ideas, was limited. Travel and trade beyond the shores of Europe and then North America has been occurring ever since. Goods and design ideas have been transported around the world, and foreign and other cultural influences became highly prized in the West.

Besides foreign design influences, designers and clients often consider use of several historic themes or cultural designs in a room or home, commonly known as eclectic design (or eclecticism). The space may combine historic themes, cultural themes, or some of several. Designers need to consider certain guidelines in order to create a successful interior for clients.

This chapter discusses some of the more commonly used other than Western cultural design influences and their application in kitchen and bathroom design. It also provides guidelines for combining several styles together, creating successful eclectic interior space.

Learning Objective 1: Identify significant architectural and interior design styles and details from another culture that are used in residential design.

Learning Objective 2: Apply design characteristics from another culture to the design of kitchens and bathrooms.

Learning Objective 3: Identify the characteristics of and create an eclectic kitchen and bathroom.

FAR EAST

In design, the term "Far East" generally refers to nations on the Asian continent from India east as well as the many island-nations that dot Asia's south and east coasts along the Pacific Ocean. Because much of this large landmass is the nation of China, it is how the nations on the Asian continent have been identified through much of history, whether they were actually part of

China or not. Occasionally India has been confused with China, although once the English gained control, its influence on design was distinguished from that of China. Japan was distinguished from China because it is an island nation, separate from the continent and, at times, more isolated. This distinction can be confusing to designers and clients alike in talking about Far East or Asian design influence. This section focuses on Japanese and Chinese influences and how they are blended in European and North American historic themes to create well-crafted, often simple rooms.

Trade with other Far Eastern countries and cultures around the world during the nineteenth and twentieth centuries grew as economies and wealth improved and worldwide communication and travel became more commonplace. Clients and designers are exposed to a great variety of design ideas that they want to incorporate into their homes. Other Far Eastern cultures have influenced Western design, but probably not as significantly or as broadly as the Chinese and Japanese cultures. The influences of other Asian countries and cultures on interior design are limited primarily to color and pattern selections as well as some characteristic motifs, accents, and accessories.

Chinese Design

A majority of the early trade beyond Europe and North America occurred with countries in the Far and Middle East. As China was the largest country in Asia/Far East, and not all Westerners understood world geography, many of the design influences were called Chinese, regardless of where they came from.

Interest in Chinese design and the desire for those goods by Europeans dates back to Marco Polo in the fourteenth century and continues to the present time. At first Europeans desired relatively small objects that were easy to transport either overland or by sailing ships, such as porcelains, lacquer ware, silks and other fabrics, hand-painted silk and paper wall coverings, and rugs. As transportation improved, larger objects and furniture of all kinds were imported to Europe and the United States.

China has been a popular design influence for Western interiors since the seventeenth century, the time of Louis XIV. This influence is usually called *chinoiserie* (the French term for "things Chinese" or "in the Chinese manner"). The Chinese style also influenced others, including the English cabinetmaker Thomas Chippendale, known for his Chinese Chippendale style. This Chinese influence continued into the nineteenth and twentieth centuries in the English Regency and Victorian styles as trade expanded and goods became available to more than just the wealthy. The Chinese style became popular again in the early twentieth century, as one of the influences on the Art Deco style. A resurgence of the Chinese style interest in the United States occurred shortly after the end of World War II when Chinese designs and furniture were featured in *House & Garden* magazine in the late 1940s and again featured in 1972 after President Nixon visited China and trade was opened up. Being featured in these widely distributed shelter magazines added interest and demand for Chinese designs, an interest that continues to the present time.

Chinese-Inspired Kitchens and Bathrooms

The cabinetry, hardware, colors, and accessories are the dominant Chinese influences used in kitchens and bathrooms. Lines typically are horizontal, with geometric shapes, including round curves. Pattern and decoration tend to be elaborate and detailed; clutter is kept to a minimum. The kitchen in Figure 7.1 shows the Chinese influence, first with the use of red and black, but also the horizontal lines of the cabinetry and most of the hardware, the round motif on some upper cabinets, and the hexagonal shape of the island, light soffit and coffer above it. In the bathroom (Figure 7.2), the cabinet is inspired by a Chinese tall cupboard used for storage.

Chinese-inspired design elements:

   Cabinetry/millwork: The design influence of Chinese cabinetry, particularly the cupboard in its many forms, is a dominant and common theme for cabinetry used in a

FIGURE 7.1 Chinese-inspired kitchen

Design by Elina Katsioula-Beall, CKD, Dewitt Designer Kitchens, Pasadena, CA
Photo by Suki Medencevic

Chinese-inspired kitchen and/or bathroom. Straight-grained, simple doors with wood graining, usually vertical, are typical. Cabinets are used to create primarily symmetrical shapes within the space. A variety of woods, from dark to light, are all appropriate in natural finishes or painted one of the typical colors, such as black or red. Some open shelves as well enclosed storage are appropriate.

Hardware/fixtures. Hardware is often a major element in the space. Brass and bronze, either shiny or burnished for handles, with plain or tooled brass faceplates, hinges, and corner brackets are typical with a matte finish. Pewter may also be used.

Countertops. Matte-finished surfaces (natural material or simulated), such as concrete, stainless steel, granite, soapstone, and wood, are typical. Oversize, thicker counters are appropriate. The backsplash area may accent the overall horizontal line with glass or ceramic tiles in a typical Chinese motif or pattern.

Floors. Concrete, wood (often worn or roughly finished recycled wood) or natural stone floors predominate. Chinese area rugs are also used.

Walls. Textured, faux-finished walls, wood-paneled or Chinese scenic wallpaper, or simply painted walls are common. Horizontal window designs with fret-carved wood frames are appropriate. Coromandel or other Chinese screens are used as room dividers.

Ceilings and lighting. Simple, classic plain white or wood ceilings predominate. A smooth-finished beam ceiling also would be appropriate in this type of environment. Brass or chrome-finished metal are used for fixtures and lighting with a brushed or matte finish.

FIGURE 7.2 Chinese-inspired bathroom cabinet

Design by Sol Quintana Wagoner, codesigners John Kavan and Vanessa Tejera, Jackson Design and Remodeling, San Diego, CA
Photo by Preview First

Colors. Typical colors are red (a red with a slight orange tinge, often called Chinese red), green, yellow, blue, black, white, and gray, tending toward pure rather than muted hues.

Representative motifs. Natural motifs, plants, and animals dominate. Calligraphy writing symbols, Chinese scenic designs, and the fret motif are also common.

Fabrics. Natural fibers, such as cotton, linen, wool, and silk, printed (the French toile de Jouy with a Chinese scenic pattern) and elaborately woven in brocades are common.

Accents/accessories. Chinese porcelains, both multicolored and blue and white, metal ware, lacquer ware, stone sculpture, Coromandel screens, and silk screens are used.

Associated styles. English and American Georgian, Arts and Crafts, Shaker, Art Nouveau, Bauhaus, Scandinavian modern, Art Deco, retro/midcentury modern, Italian/European modern, and Japanese are associated.

Japanese Design

Japan's influence on interior design, especially residential design, occurred with the reopening of trade with the island nation in the mid-nineteenth century. (Japan had been closed to all westerners except the Dutch since the middle of the seventeenth century.) This trade opening created a strong interest in the design and objects of Japanese culture, coinciding with the trend toward an appreciation of simplicity in Western design that continued into most of the twentieth century. The style became popular when much of the Western world was reacting to the elaborateness of the Victorian styles. In addition, Japanese influences worked well with Arts and Crafts and Art Nouveau styles of the late nineteenth century, as well as with the twentieth century's simple modern design styles.

The Japanese culture is global in its design interpretation. It is based on a complex contradiction of dissimilar materials and objects combined together, resulting in an environment rich in textural interest, strongly emphasizing horizontal lineal elements.

In traditional Japanese design and its many interpretations, designers admire the restrained architecture and simple interiors, focusing on presenting uncluttered elegance and functionality in a small amount of space. Over the centuries, the Japanese have developed a unique design vocabulary focusing on quiet, unpretentious objects placed in interiors so they can be individually enjoyed.

Several types of Japanese design aesthetic have been identified. Two design aesthetics, *shibui* (or *shibusa*) and *wabi-sabi*, are most often the basis of the Western interpretation and use of Japanese design in interiors. They are very similar with characteristics that overlap. Generally, designers and clients prefer and use these similar characteristics when creating interior spaces, using the umbrella name "Japanese design," rather than either more specific term.

Shibui (or *shibusa*) refers to the aesthetic of simple, subtle, unostentatious, and unobtrusive beauty, humility, and modesty, applied to a variety of subjects in life. It is considered to be the ultimate in taste. It uses irregular, asymmetrical placement and is understated, often appearing unfinished. The emphasis is on subtle details, texture rather than patterns, dull or burnished (old-looking) objects rather than shiny new ones, unobtrusive muted color with a small sharp bright color accent somewhere in the space. The ultimate aim is tranquility. *House Beautiful* magazine introduced the concept of *shibui* to American designers and consumers in its August and September 1960 issues.

Wabi-sabi refers to an aesthetic based on the acceptance of imperfection and transience. Its characteristics include asymmetry, irregularity, simplicity, economy, minimalism, and objects that are imperfect, incomplete, even unexpected. Natural objects and those that are imperfect or show their age or other signs of use are also favored. In rooms inspired by *wabi-sabi*, beautiful craftsmanship, simplicity of shape, and the juxtaposition and the resulting interplay among honest, dissimilar, unfinished, natural materials are at the heart of the design. The style is sparse, not cold but soothing, not empty but uncluttered. To paraphrase Leonard Koran, the author of *Wabi-Sabi—for Artists, Designers, Poets, & Philosophers*, the simplicity of Japanese environments is based on the ethic of creating beautiful things without getting caught up in the disparaging materialism that often surrounds creative acts.

Japanese-Inspired Kitchens and Bathrooms

Simplicity and understated design are keys to creating Japanese-inspired kitchens and bathrooms. Lines are simple, predominantly straight and with a horizontal emphasis. Clutter and decoration are kept to a minimum, with most items behind doors or in drawers, although open shelves also are used to display a select number of significant objects. Japanese design concepts work well in small spaces.

Japanese-inspired design elements:

Cabinetry/millwork. The design influence of the Japanese *tansu* chest in its many forms (or actual chests themselves) is a dominant and common theme in the cabinetry used in a Japanese-inspired kitchen and/or bathroom (see Figure 7.3). Straight-grained, simple doors with wood graining (either horizontal or vertical, or a combination of both) or inserts resembling *shoji* screen panels are also found (see Figure 7.4). Cabinets are used to create unusual asymmetrical, stepped, or angled shapes within the space. Oak, maple, cherry, recut or reconstituted veneers, and western cedar are all appropriate in natural

FIGURE 7.3 Japanese-inspired kitchen

Design by Elina Katsioula-Beall, CKD, Dewitt Designer Kitchens, Pasadena, CA
Photo by Suki Medencevic

FIGURE 7.4 Japanese-inspired bathroom
Design by Jacqueline Balint, CKD, The Kitchen Collection, Redondo Beach, CA
Larry A. Falke Photography

finishes. Often a darker wood is combined with a lighter wood to create horizontal linear interest by the interplay of woods rather than use elaborate moldings. A combination of open shelves and enclosed storage is appropriate to maintain the light, airy sense of a Japanese environment.

Hardware/fixtures. As unobtrusive as possible (counter-sunk) or a major element in the space, or a combination of both is characteristic of hardware. Black wrought iron, simple bail handles with plain or tooled wrought iron faces and corner brackets are typical with a matte finish. Wrought iron or other dark, usually black or gray finished metal is used for fixtures with a brushed or matte finish.

Countertops. Matte-finished surfaces (real material or simulated), such as concrete, stainless steel, granite, soapstone, and wood, are often used. Oversize, thicker counters and varied counter heights are appropriate. The backsplash area may accent the overall horizontal line with glass or ceramic tiles.

Floors. Concrete, wood (often worn or roughly finished recycled wood) or natural stone floors predominate. Tatami mats also are used as area rugs.

Walls. Textured, rough, faux-finished walls, wood-paneled walls (consider graining horizontally and weathered wood), or crisp, simply painted walls predominate. Horizontal window designs with wood frames are appropriate. *Shoji* screens are used as room dividers, cabinet door inserts, and as window coverings. Views to the outside garden enhance the room.

Ceilings and lighting. Simple, classic plain ceilings are common. A rustic beam ceiling also would be appropriate in this type of environment. Simple wood framed shades with rice paper, or thin, translucent glass inserts are used for lighting.

Colors. Natural, earth tone colors (from the forest, sky, or seashore), also white, off-white, or soft jade green are appropriate in subtle, muted tones. Contrast with small areas of a bright intense color or black.

Representative motifs. Natural motifs, plants, and animals dominate. Calligraphy writing symbols are also used. A strong use of textured and subtly patterned surfaces are typical as opposed to combinations of brightly colored or bold patterns.

Fabrics. Natural fibers, such as cotton, linen, wool, natural bamboo, and silk, in textures or subtle patterns are used.

Accents/accessories. Stainless steel or other burnished metal is an appropriate accent material. Wood and ceramic objects (Japanese Imari porcelain and Raku pottery, among others), silk screens, *shoji* screens, simple plant or flower arrangements such as ikebana or bonsai, and religious sculptures are used. A key is little, simple, understated ornamentation.

Associated styles: Arts and Crafts, Shaker, Art Nouveau, Bauhaus, Scandinavian modern, Art Deco, retro/midcentury modern, and postmodern are associated.

Other Kitchen and Bathroom Design Influences

With worldwide travel and trade now commonplace, design influences from other nations and cultures around the world are ongoing. Most often these design influences are colors, representative motifs/patterns, a variety of materials, and accents/accessories rather than major cabinetry, hardware, and surfacing elements. Cabinetry, hardware, lighting, and a majority of the various surfaces selections tend to follow those of the current European or Far Eastern styles, adding materials, colors, motifs, and accessories from other Far Eastern countries (Figure 7.5), or with African influence seen in Figure 7.6.

ECLECTIC DESIGN

Eclectic design (also referred to as eclecticism) combines elements or styles from several different historical periods or cultural origins within a single space to create a unique and personalized look. Many of today's consumers are interested in eclectic, personalized, unique environments with a variety of design influences that suit their interests and lifestyles. One will often see a mid-twentieth-century kitchen with a Roman Corinthian column or an Art Deco chair. Very often these more modern rooms are greatly enhanced by the addition of a treasured family piece, such as an inherited armoire or sideboard or a prized Oriental rug from travels.

However, there are certain guidelines for creating successful eclectic design. For example, in rooms where a client wants to mix and match multiple styles, identify the basic, predominant style first, then proceed from there with one or two (sometimes more) other styles used in lesser, unequal amounts. Some designers have proposed various formulas to use in determining the amounts of each style to use, but a good rule of thumb is the dominant style be more than half (anywhere from 60 to 70 percent); the next style 20 to 40 percent; and if there is a third (or fourth) style, about 10 percent. Using more than three distinct styles in the same space without much thought or plan can create a cluttered, disorganized room. However, if some of the design elements (discussed in Chapter 3) are similar, that can tie different styles together to create an interesting, unique, and successful room.

Four ways to introduce eclectic design are discussed next.

FIGURE 7.5 Other cultural influences, Far East

Design by Jaque Bethke, codesigner Amy Medler, Pure Design Environments, Eden Prairie, MN
Photo by Jill Greer/Greer Photo

FIGURE 7.6 Other cultural influences, Africa

Design by Elina Katsioula-Beall, CKD, Dewitt Designer Kitchens, Pasadena, CA
Photo by Suki Medencevic

Enhancing a New Kitchen or Bathroom with Old Objects

The most typical way eclectic design is applied within a kitchen or bathroom space is by adding some objects from a different era or even culture into a new space. A unique vitality is added to the space that embraces the present, the past, the future, or far away culture in one sweeping view. For example, a more modern/twentieth-century environment favoring simple visual restraint is more interesting with the addition of a reference to past times as its focal point: a single piece of antique or iconic furniture or vintage plumbing fixtures with otherwise contemporary cabinetry and lighting fixtures (see Figures 7.7 and 7.8). This unexpected contrast between new and old accentuates the difference, allowing those enjoying the space to celebrate both what was and what is.

Placing a New Kitchen or Bathroom within an Old Setting

Eclectic enthusiasts realize that the historic architecture of the home is not compromised if the interior has transitions into one or more modern rooms. City loft living spaces, often in converted warehouses from a bygone era, are great examples of this. A modern European/ Italian kitchen design may be seen against old brick walls and a well-worn wide-plank wood floor, with furniture and/or objects displayed from the client's travels or family collection. Figure 7.9 is an example of this with a kitchen in a converted warehouse loft space, with the worn brick wall, contemporary cabinetry and seating, and a vintage popcorn machine.

FIGURE 7.7 Eclectic-style kitchen, vintage and contemporary combined
Design by Lauren Levant Bland, Jennifer Gilmer Kitchen & Bath Ltd., Chevy Chase, MD
Photo by Bob Narod, Photographer, LLC

FIGURE 7.8 Eclectic-style bathroom, vintage and contemporary combined

Design by Chris Berry, codesigner Susie Knopf, Brooks Berry Kitchens and Baths, St. Louis, MO
Photo by Alise O'Brien Photography

FIGURE 7.9 Eclectic design—a new kitchen in a converted warehouse space
Courtesy of Wood-Mode Fine Custom Cabinetry

Collector's Mix

A collector's kitchen or bathroom interior includes objects treasured and unique to the client, and falls into one of three broad categories:

1. **Overall aesthetic of abundance.** This approach can be summed up as planned clutter, with numerous groupings, ideally of similarly styled objects, on nearly every space and surface.
2. **Artistic presentation.** Other collectors prefer interiors with a gallerylike quality: edited backgrounds that allow one or more collections to be undisputedly in the forefront (see Figures 7.10 and 7.11).
3. **Cross-cultural mix.** Some eclectic environments today combine elements from different cultures or historic time periods—the room expresses the owner's personal journey through time and to new places. Cross-cultural eclecticism may be based around an important architectural element found during the client's travels: a massive stone table, for example, from the Tuscan region; artwork, glassware, or other treasured objects from travels showcased in an otherwise uncluttered room (see Figure 7.12).

Signature Element

Some interiors, like individuals, have a particular identifying characteristic that sets them apart from others. A signature element may take center stage in the space, with the designer using

FIGURE 7.10 Artistic presentation of a collection—kitchen cabinetry display

Design by Lilley E. Yee, CMKBD, CID, ASID, Lilley Yee Interiors, San Mateo, CA
Photography Copyright © Dean J. Birinyi, ASMP

FIGURE 7.11 An artistic presentation of a collection—bathroom display

Design by Sol Quintana Wagoner, codesigners John Kavan and Vanessa Tejera, Jackson Design and Remodeling, San Diego, CA
Photo by Preview First

FIGURE 7.12 Eclectic design—A cross-cultural mix of objects

Design by Karen Black, A Karen Black Company, Oklahoma City, OK
Photo by Photoart Studios

FIGURE 7.13 Eclectic kitchen design—Signature element, art work display

Design by Tim Scott, codesigners Erica Westeroth CKD, NCIDQ, and Sheena Hammond, XTC Design Inc., Toronto, ON
Photo by Larry Arnal—Arnal Photography

elements of design (line and form, texture and pattern, color and light) to allow that signature item (or items) to be boldly and clearly the focal point within the overall room, such as the paintings in the kitchen in Figure 7.13.

SUMMARY

This chapter discusses selected cultural influences, primarily those from the Far East, that are most frequently being used in the design of kitchens and bathrooms. Aspects of eclectic design, including some guidelines for designers and examples of its application in these settings are also covered.

REVIEW QUESTIONS

1. Identify the significant architectural and interior design styles and details from the Far East that are used in residential design. (See "Far East" pages 189–190)
2. Identify design characteristics from Japanese design used in kitchens and bathrooms. (See "Japanese Design"pages193–196)
3. Identify design characteristics from Chinese design used in kitchens and bathrooms. (See "Chinese Design" pages 190–193)
4. Identify the characteristics of eclectic design in kitchens and bathrooms. (See "Eclectic Design" page 196)

Theme/Historic Styles Compatibility

The following chart is meant to serve only as a guide to assist the designer when working with clients and considering design styles for spaces. Most spaces combine several style influences, whether they are similar or diverse. There is no right or wrong (not everyone agrees); it depends on what the client wants and the designer puts together. People can combine any and as many styles as they like, as reflect their lifestyle and personality, and as they feel comfortable with. Feel free to do so. When diverse styles are used in the same space, the interior typically is called eclectic. It is good to keep in mind that one style usually dominates in a well-designed space; other styles are then used in lesser, mostly unequal amounts.

Major Period or Cultural Style	Generally Compatible With
Ancient classical styles of Greece and Rome	Renaissance, Baroque, Georgian, Neoclassic styles of the eighteenth and nineteenth centuries, Art Deco, postmodern (late twentieth century), any style that uses classical design motifs
Middle Ages/Gothic	All Renaissance styles, English Tudor and Jacobean, any English and American country style, Chippendale Gothick, Victorian Gothic revival, Arts and Crafts
Old World/Renaissance styles (Italian and Tuscan, Spanish, English)	Baroque, Victorian Renaissance revival, Gothic, English Tudor and Jacobean, English and American country styles, ancient Greek and Roman
Baroque styles	Renaissance styles, eighteenth-century Georgian, Rococo, Victorian Renaissance revival
Rococo/French provincial	Seventeenth- and eighteenth-century English and American country styles, Biedermeier, Art Nouveau, Victorian Rococo, Swedish neoclassic
Eighteenth-century Georgian	Any eighteenth- and early nineteenth-century Neoclassic style, Baroque, Rococo, French provincial, Chinese
American colonial	Renaissance, English Tudor and Jacobean, French provincial, Gothic, English Georgian, Shaker, any other country styles

(continued)

Major Period or Cultural Style	Generally Compatible With
Shaker	American colonial, Arts and Crafts, twentieth-century Scandinavian modern, all late twentieth-century styles, Japanese
Spanish Mission	Renaissance, especially Spanish, also Italian, Arts and Crafts, Native American, influences from Mexico and Central and South America
Neoclassic (end of eighteenth, early nineteenth century, English, French, American)	Eighteenth-century Georgian styles, Biedermeier, all other Neoclassic styles, ancient Greek and Roman, twentieth-century Postmodern
Swedish Neoclassic	English, French, and American Neoclassic styles; Biedermeier; twentieth-century Scandinavian; Shaker
Biedermeier	English, French, and American Neoclassic styles; Art Deco; contemporary Scandinavian styles
Victorian styles (nineteenth century)	Gothic, Renaissance, Baroque, Rococo, Georgian, Chinese, Japanese, Middle Eastern styles
Arts and Crafts	Renaissance, Gothic, Shaker, Spanish Mission, Art Nouveau, Japanese, Chinese, Native American
Art Nouveau	French Rococo, Art Deco, Japanese, Arts and Crafts
Art Deco	Art Nouveau, Japanese, Arts and Crafts, Bauhaus, twentieth-century Scandinavian, midcentury modern, late twentieth-century postmodern
Bauhaus (international modern)	Art Deco, Arts and Crafts (especially work of Frank Lloyd Wright), Scandinavian modern, midcentury modern, postmodern, Italian and European modern
Scandinavian modern	Art Deco, Arts and Crafts (especially work of Frank Lloyd Wright), Bauhaus, midcentury modern, postmodern, Italian and European Modern, Biedermeier, Swedish Neoclassic, Shaker
Midcentury modern (Retro)	Art Deco, Arts and Crafts, Bauhaus, Scandinavian modern, Shaker, postmodern
Italian and European modern (since the 1950s)	Art Deco, Arts and Crafts, Bauhaus, Scandinavian modern, Shaker and other country styles, midcentury modern, postmodern, Japanese
Postmodern (1970s and 1980s)	Ancient Greek and Roman, Art Deco, Arts and Crafts, Bauhaus, Scandinavian modern, Shaker, midcentury modern, Japanese
Japanese	Arts and Crafts, Shaker, Art Nouveau, Bauhaus, Scandinavian modern, Art Deco, midcentury modern, Italian and European modern, Chinese
Chinese	English and American Georgian, Arts and Crafts, Shaker, Art Nouveau, Bauhaus, Scandinavian modern, Art Deco, midcentury modern, Italian and European modern, Japanese

APPENDIX
Historical Terminology and Themes

When embarking on an overview of the history of architecture and of interior and furniture design, one needs to become familiar with the terminology used. The following is a list of selected terms. Numerous architecture and interior design–specific dictionaries are available for reference for additional terms and definitions. A word of caution: Often there are multiple definitions and interpretations for the same term. There also are several terms with the same or very similar definitions that are used interchangeably. Knowing the context in which a term is used is important to understanding and interpreting with the correct meaning. The more specific terms are primarily used in academia, while the broad, more general terms are used more frequently by consumers, designers, manufacturers, and others in the industry.

As one studies the history of architecture and understands the homes of the United States, specific periods of design and styles of furniture will be identified. These eras are commonly called *period styles*.

Classic (Classical): In Western design, classic generally refers to the architecture, design, elements, and motifs of the ancient Greeks and Romans and those later styles that include them. Classic also refers to design and elements with an established acceptance and degree of excellence that has endured, stood the test of time, and remained appropriate.

Examples of classic or classically inspired styles:

Greek

Roman

Italian Renaissance

Eighteenth-century Georgian

Federal, Empire styles, Biedermeier

Colonial: Generally refers to the colonies (in this volume, the original 13 British colonies of the United States) and item or items of a colony. These are usually simplified versions of more elaborate original styles of the colonizing country, or a combination of cultural elements, typically English, French, Dutch, Spanish, and German influences found in the United States during the colonial periods (seventeenth and eighteenth centuries).

Examples of Colonial styles:

Shaker

American country

Pilgrim

American versions of seventeenth- and eighteenth-century English styles

Spanish Mission

Pennsylvania Dutch (German)

Contemporary (also referred to as modern): A look that reflects the design trends of the present-day society. Today, this design combines styles from recent diverse periods and cultures as well as new design trends and innovations. This term can be confusing, as some people use the terms interchangeably and to refer to all the periods and styles since the beginning of the twentieth century until the present time. Most often, the terms "contemporary" and "modern" refer to those styles common and popular after World War II.

Examples of contemporary or modern styles:

Midcentury modern

International modern (Bauhaus)

Scandinavian or Danish modern

Italian or European modern

Postmodern

Country (also referred to as provincial, colonial, rural, or rustic): Styles that are found in rural areas, out in the country, or in small towns and villages, as distinguished from urban styles or those found in large cities. The term is used most often to define a simpler, informal, more casual style adapted from the more elaborate city style of a particular country. When incorporating characteristics unique to a region, the term "country" can also be considered vernacular. Many formal styles have a simplified country or provincial version.

Examples of common country styles:

Shaker

French provincial (or French country)

Spanish Mission

English country

Scandinavian country

Eclectic/Eclecticism: A style composed of elements drawn from a variety of historical periods, cultures, and styles. Eclecticism refers to the use of mixing of elements from several different styles and/or periods in the same space.

Midcentury modern: A term identifying the postwar 1950 into 1960s design era, which focused on using new building materials, shapes, and colors within modern environments. An experimental time in the architectural and industrial design world.

Motif: A recurring, salient, thematic design element or feature. A motif may be a pattern, design, emblem, or object that is characteristically associated with a particular style, often several styles.

Neoclassic: "New classic." Generally refers to the late eighteenth-, early nineteenth-century architecture and design elements, primarily in France, England, and the United States, based on ancient Greek and Roman elements. This style arose after the discovery of the ruins at Pompeii and Herculaneum.

Examples of Neoclassic styles:

French Louis XVI

French Directoire

French and American Empire

American Federal

English Regency

Biedermeier

Old World: In North America, a term used by designers and the industry to describe design details from European countries, notably the English, Italian, and French country homes from the pre-Renaissance through the eighteenth century.

Examples of Old World styles:

Italian Tuscan

English country

French country

Period: Defines a particular time cycle, era, or series of events in architectural and design history when a design style prevailed.

Style: A distinctive quality, form, or type of architecture or design with its own typical characteristics.

Traditional: Refers to designs from past generations that have established, recognizable, and enduring characteristics and style, usually the more formal versions of the large cities. In North America, the term is often used to describe the architecture and formal interiors and furnishings from the late seventeenth, primarily eighteenth, and early nineteenth centuries with origins in Europe, primarily France and England that remain popular today (i.e., they never seem to go out of style).

Examples of traditional styles:

Queen Anne

Chippendale

Georgian

French Louis XV and Louis XVI

French and American Empire

Transitional: A term used to describe a style (interior, architecture, or furniture) that combines the elements of an existing style with elements of an emerging, new style. "Transitional" signifies a passage or evolution from one style to another, which is gradual over time.

Vernacular: The localized adaptation of a formal style from the cities, exhibiting notable ethnic and regional interpretations—usually in rural or provincial areas.

Victorian: Refers to the several styles, mostly revivals of earlier styles, that were popular and predominant during the reign of Queen Victoria (roughly the entire nineteenth century) and mainly found in England and the United States.

TYPES OF HISTORIC DESIGN PROJECTS

A variety of terms is used to describe the type of historic or theme design project. It is important to understand what each term means (there are subtle differences), as many are used interchangeably and could be misinterpreted by both clients as well as design and building professionals. A clear understanding by all parties involved is critical to a successful design project.

Remodel: The broad term used to describe any kind of change to an existing structure. Usually involves structural changes, often a change in use or function. It can an be a rearrangement of existing space or an addition of space. Does not necessarily but could involve renovation or restoration.

Renovation: A more specific term defined as making something existing new, updating what was there. Other similar terms in use are "restyling" or "modernizing." This is what is commonly done for kitchens and bathrooms to update them and not necessarily keep the theme or style of the structure.

Restoration: Another specific term defined as wanting to restore the space and objects in it to the previous or original condition (as closely as possible), often to the style as well as feeling of the era in which the home was built. An especially popular trend for kitchen and bathroom projects is returning to one of the earlier styles from the twentieth century, which may have been original to the house.

Re-creation: The term generally used for a completely new structure (inside and out) that is built either to replicate as closely as possible a style from the past (such as many of the structures in Colonial Williamsburg) or to give a feeling of an earlier style era, as with some recent completely new-built residential construction. Architecture, floor plan, colors, materials, and finishes that replicate or are close to what would have been in an original structure are used, but with modern amenities and code requirements.

Resources

There are many publications and websites that go into great detail on the history of interior design and architecture, more so than covered in this volume. Following is a selected list of helpful references (there are many more) for those interested in further information and study in this area in general, kitchens and bathroom design, or on a specific style or period. Several of the websites listed are specific to a particular style or time period. Many are the websites of print periodicals and include recent articles and photos, as well as archives of past issues. Other sites are designers' own websites created to show the consumer examples of good design and their own design work. Not included are the websites of numerous manufacturers of materials and products for historic design as well as design blogs that are also potential sources of design inspiration. These, as with websites, are numerous and come and go frequently with new ones added all the time. These are places to start.

DICTIONARIES OF INTERIOR DESIGN

Allen Dizik, *Concise Encyclopedia of Interior Design* (2nd ed.) (New York: Van Nostrand Reinhold, 1988).

Mark Hinchman, *The Fairchild Books Dictionary of Interior Design* (3rd ed.) (New York: Fairchild Books, 2013).

Frederic H. Jones, *The Concise Dictionary of Interior Design* (Concise Dictionary Series) (Los Altos, CA: Crisp Publications, 1990).

Martin M. Pegler, *The Dictionary of Interior Design* (New York: Fairchild Publications, 1983).

Josette H. Rabun, Catherine L. Kendall, and Julie L. Rabun, *The Anglicized and Illustrated Dictionary of Interior Design* (Boston: Pearson, 2013).

HISTORIC ARCHITECTURE, INTERIORS, AND FURNITURE

Stanley Abercrombie and Sherrill Whiton, *Interior Design and Decoration* (6th ed.) (Upper Saddle River, NJ: Pearson Prentice Hall, 2008).

Robbie G. Blakemore, *History of Interior Design and Furniture: From Ancient Egypt to Nineteenth-Century Europe* (2nd ed.) (Hoboken, NJ: John Wiley and Sons, 2006).

Stephen Calloway, *The Elements of Style: A Practical Encyclopedia of Interior Architectural Details from 1485 to the Present* (revised edition) (New York: Simon and Schuster, 1996).

Francis D. K. Ching *A Visual Dictionary of Architecture* (2nd ed.) (Hoboken, NJ: John Wiley and Sons, 2012).

Francis D. K. Ching and Corky Binggeli, *Interior Design Illustrated* (3rd ed.) (Hoboken, NJ: John Wiley and Sons, 2012).

Kathleen Donohue, *Kitchen and Bath Theme Design: An Architectural Styling Guide* (New York: McGraw-Hill, 1999).

Michelle Gringeri-Brown and Jim Brown, *Atomic Ranch: Design Ideas for Stylish Ranch Homes* (Layton, UT: Gibbs Smith, 2006).

———. *Atomic Ranch Midcentury Interiors* (Layton, UT: Gibbs Smith, 2012).

Buie Harwood, Bridget May, and Curt Sherman, *Architecture and Interior Design: An Integrated History to the Present* (Boston: Prentice Hall, 2012).

Jeannie Ireland, *History of Interior Design* (New York: Fairchild Books, 2009).

Virginia and Lee McAlester, *A Field Guide to American Houses* (New York: Alfred A. Knopf, 1984); second edition by Virginia Savage McAlester (New York: Alfred A. Knopf, 2013).

John Pile and Judith Gura, *History of Interior Design* (4th ed.) (Hoboken, NJ: John Wiley and Sons, 2014).

Jane Powell and Linda Svendsen, *Bungalow Kitchens* (Salt Lake City, UT: Gibbs Smith, 2000).

———. *Bungalow Bathrooms (Bungalow Basics)* (Salt Lake City, UT: Gibbs Smith, 2001).

Mario Praz, *An Illustrated History of Interior Decoration: From Pompeii to Art Nouveau* (London: Thames and Hudson, 1981).

Bradley Quinn, *Mid-Century Modern: Interiors, Furniture, Design Details* (Conran Octopus Interiors) (London: Conran, 2006).

Esther Schmidt and Franklin Schmidt, *Victorian Kitchens and Baths* (Salt Lake City, UT: Gibbs Smith, 2005; Kindle edition 2011).

William B. Tuthill, *Late Victorian Interiors and Interior Details* (Dover Architecture) (Mineola, NY: Dover Publications, 2010).

RENOVATION, PRESERVATION, AND RESTORATION

Frank Shirley Architects and the National Trust for Historic Preservation, *New Rooms for Old Houses: Beautiful Additions for the Traditional Home* (Newtown, CT: Taunton Press, 2007).

Peter B. Dedek, *Historic Preservation for Designers* (New York: Fairchild Books, 2013).

Aaron Lubeck, *Green Restorations: Sustainable Building and Historic Homes* (Gabriola Island, BC: New Society Publishers, 2010).

George Nash, *Renovating Old Houses: Bringing New Life to Vintage Homes* (Newtown, CT: Taunton Press, 2003).

Russell Versaci and the American Institute of Architects, *Creating a New Old House: Yesterday's Character for Today's Home* (Newtown, CT: Taunton Press, 2007).

HISTORIC AND GLOBAL COLOR

Faber Birren, *Color for Interiors: Historical and Modern* (New York: Whitney Library of Design, 1963).

Leatrice Eiseman and Keith Recker, *Pantone: The Twentieth Century in Color* (San Francisco: Chronicle Books, 2011).

Augustine Hope and Margaret Walch, *Living Colors: The Definitive Guide to Color Palettes through the Ages* by (San Francisco: Chronicle Books, 2002).

Jean-Philippe Lenclos and Dominique Lenclos, *Colors of the World: A Geography of Color* (Gregory P. Bruhn, trans.) (New York: W. W. Norton and Co., 2004).

SELECTED WEBSITES

www.modernbungalow.com

www.oldhouseweb.com

www.oldhouseonline.com

www.oldhousejournal.com

www.thisoldhouse.com

www.finehomebuilding.com

www.retrorenovation.com

www.atomic-ranch.com

www.dwell.com

www.metropolismag.com

www.houzz.com

www.pinterest.com

www.hgtv.com

www.apartmenttherapy.com

www.bradbury.com

www.bobvilla.com

www.preservation.org

Index

If you enjoyed this book, you may also like these:

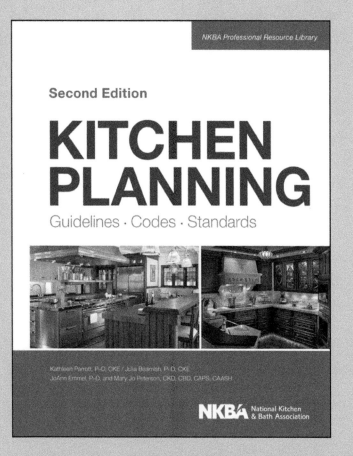

Kitchen Planning 2e
by Kathleen Parrott, Julia Beamish, JoAnn Emmel,
and Mary Jo Peterson
ISBN: 9781118367629

Bath Planning 2e
by Kathleen Parrott, Julia Beamish, JoAnn Emmel,
and Mary Jo Peterson
ISBN: 9781118362488